UNIX
as a Second Language

UNIX Systems Management
for
Mainframe Systems Professionals

Robert H. (Bob) Johnson

D1402066

UNIX as a Second Language

The information presented in *UNIX as a Second Language* is subject to change. Comments may be addressed to:

Landmark Systems Corporation
8000 Towers Crescent Drive
Vienna, Virginia 22182-2700

1- 800-775-LMRK (1-800-775-5675)
1-703-902-8000

Edition Date ....September 1996
USL-09/96

Landmark Systems Corporation and the Landmark logo, NaviGraph, **The Monitor** for CICS, **The Monitor** for MVS, **The Monitor** for VSE, and their logos, and NaviGate, Pinnacle, PROBE/Net, and PROBE/X are registered trademarks; and NaviPlex, Performance Series for MVS, Performance Series for UNIX, Performance Series for VSE, *PerformanceWorks*, **The Monitor** for DB2, **The Monitor** for Sybase, **The Monitor** for UNIX, **The Monitor** for VTAM, and their logos, and the Pinnacle, PROBE/Net, and PROBE/X logos are trademarks of Landmark Systems Corporation.

UNIX is a registered trademark in the United States and other countries licensed exclusively through X/Open Company, Ltd. All other product and brand names mentioned are trademarks or registered trademarks of their respective holders.

Contents

PART III: Systems Management

Part IV: Appendixes

Glossary

Index

LANDM▲RK

Preface

Why did I pick *UNIX as a Second Language* as the title and *UNIX Systems Management for Mainframe Systems Professionals* as the subtitle of this book? Why does the cover have a butterfly on it? (No, the reason is not that I want to imitate the O'Reily series of animal books!) Then why?

Computing for the rest of the 1990s and into the 21st century requires the appropriate platform for enterprise computing. We have already seen over a decade of personal computers providing a platform for successful individual computing. Today UNIX is taking its place in distributed, intermediate-sized, departmentwide computing.

I have written this book because I believe that hundreds of thousands of mainframe systems professionals have a lot in common with the open systems folks. If the two groups could understand each other's languages, they might work better as a team toward achieving corporate computing goals.

If you are an IBM mainframe-based person who wants to learn to manage (or maybe just spell) UNIX, this book presents systems management concepts in your language and shows you the differences and similarities between MVS and UNIX. Even more important, OpenEdition MVS provides a more standard UNIX system support than many of the other UNIX systems. As of this writing, OS/390 (the name of MVS today is applying for UNIX/95 certification.

If you are a UNIX-based person who is trying to learn from the wealth of systems management philosophies in the mainframe environment, this work shows you what the equivalents are in your environment.

Now to the butterfly. Butterflies represent a new beginning: from egg to caterpillar to chrysalis to butterfly. It fits for two reasons. First, the butterfly represents a new beginning for mainframe professionals. Second, the first port of UNIX to a really new platform was done in 1976 by Richard Miller at the University of Wollongong, south of Sydney, Australia. I took this butterfly's picture in the woods (not "rain-forest") in Kuranda, Australia. (Ok, that is NORTH of Sydney.) The butterfly is a brilliant blue swallowtail subspecies of Paplio Ulysses.

So how does the butterfly fit in here? Information technology (IT) organizations are changing from a worm to a butterfly! Many successful organizations are moving from a vertical organization (MVS/VM/VSE operating systems, database, and OLTP under one manager) to a horizontal organization (mainframe operating systems and UNIX, DB2 with Sybase and Oracle, and CICS on all platforms with a manager for each discipline). This means that corporations are assigning technicians to *fix* information processing no matter what their backgrounds happen to be. In other words, IT is moving toward providing products and services to their "customers" and helping them solve problems, not just give them technology.

Each of us, as part of the data processing environment, must join together to implement the Age of Information. That is what "AI" really means, not just artificial intelligence. Who needs artificial intelligence anyway? We need *real* intelligence! As Benjamin Franklin said, "If we don't hang together, we will surely hang separately." That is as true today as it was in revolutionary times, only instead of hanging, we will be out of a job or our businesses will fail.

A Word on the Style Used

I have kept this book simple, introducing complex topics in general terms at the beginning and building on your understanding of those topics. I have used this approach successfully in earlier books and continue it here. The UNIX world has a large number of great books that explain the components. Several are mentioned at the end of this preface.

This book is about the operating system components. Relational database systems (such as Sybase and Oracle) are an important part of both platforms but beyond the scope of this book.

What You Need To Know To Read this Book

This book is an introduction to MVS and UNIX and assumes that you, as the reader, do not have detailed knowledge of all pieces of the architectures of the two systems. You should either be "in the business" or be studying to be "in the business."

Be sure to check the documentation provided with your operating system and be sure it matches the version of the system you are running. In the mainframe environment, things change rapidly. In the open systems environment, they change hourly.

Acknowledgments

A large number of colleagues assisted with input to this work. Jim Marshall was the first of many. His insights were most helpful to clarify the basic concepts. Dr. Rich Olcott provided a wealth of comments and proved again his technical expertise and his friendship. Douglas Clapp provided much-needed technical editing.

As usual, a large contingency from Landmark were downright vital to this work. It is great working at a company with so many dedicated, smart, and experienced experts in operating systems, database, multiplatform, and performance and tuning disciplines. Bill Clothier and Craig Stone provided insight on the VSE and VM portions. Members of the Technical Communications staff (Sarah Abrams, Mary Apple, Penny Garver, Gina Karpathakis, Jennifer Khoury, Kelly LeBoeuf, Jeri McDuffee, Anne Reaver, Glenn Sartori, and Sarah Frey Swett) were particularly helpful. Penny did a super job editing this work. If it reads smoothly and clearly communicates, she gets the credit. If there are problems, I must not have made her changes! Mary completely rewrote the SCSI chapter and the "wire" part was moved to the appendix to get it out of the way of the real meat of tuning UNIX channels. Sarah Swett is the technical writer for *PerformanceWorks* for UNIX and added to the tuning information.

Ed Gray did much of the research for the security chapter. Heather Dickman either created or added to the figures. Steve Sonnenberg provided a great introduction to UNIX metrics. Joe Berry, who co-authored the PROBE products, gave me my start in understanding the metrics one can obtain from the UNIX environment. Craig Despeaux in the quality assurance lab helped me translate from mainframe to UNIX. Jim Peterson added great value to my view of operating systems. Charlie Wade came on as a systems engineer and provided great insight to tuning UNIX. His background with Storage Technology Corporation (STC) was a vital part of our understanding of SCSI channels. Jeff Johnson added his wonderful hardware knowledge to my toolbox.

Once again my friend, Randy Chalfant, was a catalyst for me to expand this book into what it has become. Randy is one of the few individuals who can look at a leaf on a tree and see the forest around him. Not only that, he can explain the breadth and depth of the forest!

My son, R. Daniel Johnson, who has been a co-author and master reviewer, added much to this work because he was a distributed systems programmer for over a decade and provided much from real-life situations. He was particularly helpful with the I/O, security, and tuning portions as he started using Multics at Honeywell during high school.

I am astounded at the friends that I have who were there when all of this was happening. While I was slugging it out in the data centers of government and private industry, a large number of my contemporaries were at MIT, Bell Labs, and/or IBM. Bill Malik of the Gartner Group provided wonderful insights into the world of UNIX and the mainframe. Bill wins the "most information provided" award. He is almost as good a technical reviewer as I can be on my best day! Bernie "Dr. Death" Domanski admitted to me that he wrote the original SAR routines. Dr. Pat Artis was there, too!

May the Source Be with You

The background for the MVS environment comes from my research for *MVS Concepts and Facilities*, by Robert H. Johnson (McGraw-Hill, 1989, ISBN 0-07-032673-8; Spanish McGraw-Hill, 1993, ISBN 84-481-0092-1) and *DASD: IBM's Direct Access Storage Devices*, by Robert H. and R. Daniel Johnson (McGraw-Hill, 1991, ISBN 0-07-032674-6) and is included with permission.

My education on UNIX began with, and I am deeply grateful to the folks at, O'Reiley & Associates. They gathered a wealth of UNIX knowledge and published it for the world to see. Some of their books I used in my research were *The Design of the UNIX Operating System* by Maurice J. Bach (ISBN 0-13-201799-7), *System Performance Tuning* by Mike Loukides (ISBN 0-93-7175-60-9), *Essential System Administration* by Aeleen Frisch (ISBN 0-937175-80-3), and *Practical UNIX Security* by Simson Garfinkle and Gene Spafford (ISBN 0-937175-72-2).

Other publishers contribute to our base of knowledge. *The Magic Garden Explained* by Berny Goodheart and James Cox (ISBN 0-13-098138-9) gives an excellent operating systems viewpoint (as Berny said to me in Australia, "The magic never stops!"). *Firewalls and Internet Security* by William R. Cheswick and Steven M. Bellovin (ISBN 0-201-63357-4 Addison-Wesley) gives a good introduction to security. *Sun Performance and Tuning* by Adrian Cockcroft (ISBN 0-13-149642-5) gives practical and very specific things to do to make your SUN systems run better. *The UNIX Operating System* (ISBN 0-471-58684-6) by Kaare Christian and Susan Richter is a good overall guide and very useful for commands.

Mark Friedman (Demand Technology, Inc. at 800-531-6143) and his *Storage Management Newsletter* provide an up-to-date source of information and techniques. It is a "must-read" publication in a sea of data!

Cheryl Watson (*Cheryl Watson's Tuning Letter* at 800-553-4562) provides many tuning tips and terms, especially for Open Edition (UNIX on the mainframe).

Finally, for the real low-down on the Internet, see Cliff Stoll's *Silicon Snake Oil* (Doubleday, ISBN 0-385-41993-7).

Note To Readers

September 1996: This is a work-in-progress. Your input is solicited and will be greatly appreciated. If you have corrections, additions, samples, or other information you think would be valuable to the translation process, please forward them to me. If you wish, you will be added to a list of contributing authors (you know, no money, but a title on the door!). Thank you for your help in advance.

Another thing — jump in. If I can collect this information and publish it, you can, too. On several occasions, as I have sent out chapters to be reviewed to systems administrators, I have gotten back requests for 30 or more copies of the draft manuscript. Upon query, the person said something like "The book is so complete and it provides so much needed information, I wanted to give it to all of the people in the distributed department." While that is flattering to me, it didn't advance the information available to the world. Dig in and criticize not only my work but the work of any person *writing* about data processing.

That's how we have gotten as far as we have — by sharing what we know.

Disclaimer

The information in this book is provided on an as-is basis without any warranty either expressed or implied. The use of this information or the implementation of any of these techniques is your responsibility and depends on your ability to evaluate and integrate them into your environment.

Introduction

I believe that you can describe the corporate data processing environment as a triad of computing. Webster's Dictionary defines a *triad* as "a union or group of three." A three-legged stool comes to mind. Without one of the three legs, the seat is very unstable. Shortening one of the legs (*downsizing*) must be done carefully or you will have no seat to sit on! Growing one leg out of proportion to the others also may be painful. Sometimes a *unipod* (for example, just mainframes) is just what is needed, but at the end of the day, balance is what is usually called for.

My definition of the *triad of computing* is *centralized processing* in the form of mainframes; *decentralized distributed processing* using UNIX, AS/400, or Tandem-like computers; and *desktop computing* using personal computers or powerful small systems (for example, Sun workstations or IBM's RS/6000). I have believed in and implemented this triad for over a decade.

The over-used term *client/server* does not fit into this definition. Client/server is an architectural model, not a platform. Work is performed on one platform cooperatively with another to perform useful work. You could say that CICS (terminal access and security) accessing DB2 or IMS files (databases) is a client/server system. You could also consider the CICS terminal-owning region (TOR) a client and the CICS file-owning region (FOR) a server.

I believe every medium-to-large company should have this triad of computing in their strategic plan! I will go even further: Unless companies have real, well thought-out, documented reasons not to include the triad, they are doing their companies a real disservice by limiting their processing to just one or two of these legs.

This work is a tutorial on the architecture and tuning of mainframe and distributed systems in general. The two environments are very similar, using different names for comparable components. The work focuses on the performance management aspect of the broader systems management philosophy of computing.

The mainframe is described using MVS/ESA as an example. Virtual Machine/Enterprise Systems Architecture (VM/ESA) and VSE/ESA differences are noted where significant. Distributed computing is described using UNIX and is explained from a vendor-independent environment and generally applies to the System V implementation. HP, IBM/AIX, SCO, and Sun platforms are highlighted. Practical examples are presented for both platforms, contrasting the two architectures.

UNIX is really a *scalable operating system.* You can run UNIX on a very small processor complex. You don't even need disk (*DASD* to mainframe people) or tape. All of the accesses can be via networks. Try running MVS, VM, VSE, or even AS/400 operating systems without a gaggle of DASD. You should not be surprised that UNIX does not start with systems management in mind. Security and I/O considerations are going to be primitive. (Hold your horses, those of you who are UNIX systems administrators. I'll describe how to make UNIX secure.)

What Is Included

All of old-world Gaul was divided into three parts. So it is with performance of computers and this book. You have only three computer components to worry about from the performance management perspective: the central processing unit (CPU), input/output (I/O), and processor storage. The devil is in the details!

Part I discusses genealogy and architecture and lays a general foundation for the rest of the chapters. It is not designed as a comprehensive work, as both MVS and UNIX operating systems and the hardware architectures they run on are thoroughly documented in other referenced books.

Part II compares the three computer components. The CPU is first, because it is vital for the operating system to be configured to give CPU resources to the most important tasks in your company. Second is processor storage for the same reason. Storage is important because, when an operating system develops storage problems, it starts thrashing and makes the problems even worse. Finally, the real meat of understanding and tuning an operating system is the I/O system. Nothing causes the agony and the ecstasy the I/O system causes. When it is running well, it is a thing to behold. When it is operating poorly, you can't get a handle on it at all.

Part III discusses systems management on the two platforms. Security is a focal point because the security and reliability of data is vital in this era of the information highway. A discussion of tuning topics is included to give you enterprisewide performance management perspectives.

Appendix A is a translation dictionary for mainframe and distributed terms. It is designed for you to look up a term you are comfortable with in one environment and see what its "equivalent" is in the other environment. Remember to look in the index for other places the term is referenced in the text. Appendix B is a guide to the desktop and distributed environment's device architecture. Finally a glossary of distributed terms is included.

LANDM▲RK

Part I: Genealogy and Architecture

The first part of the book is designed to show how the two operating systems and their platforms have grown over almost three decades. In the '70s, a movie, *Deliverance*, came out about a group of four men going on the last whitewater canoe trip down a river before a dam is to be built, flooding the valley. One of the most memorable scenes is when the four come to a town upstream to hire guides to take the cars the many miles down to the end of the trip. During the negotiations, one of the campers starts playing his guitar in response to a young retarded boy on the porch playing a banjo. The boy teaches his song to the camper. The resultant song, *Dueling Banjos*, is a classic.

Ned Beatty, one of the actors, makes a bigoted comment about the boy, something like "a clear case of genetic deficiency." Unless you are watching closely, you miss the point at which the boy beats the camper in the "duel." The city slicker gives up.

If you are able to get beyond the violence and bigotry Hollywood so often mistakes for art, there is a lesson in this scene for us in the computer industry. Some of my mainframe friends make such remarks about UNIX as a platform. Some of my UNIX friends make such comments about the mainframe platform.

Mainframe and UNIX platforms should not be caught in a duel. They should provide beautiful music together for our customers.

Chapter 1: Genealogy

One normally thinks of genealogy in terms of human or animal history. I strongly believe that knowing the "heredity" of computing systems is as important to understanding them as knowing the "heredity" of people is to understanding human existence.

1.1 Mainframe Genealogy

Some of us in the mainframe world know and love our operating systems. We cut our teeth on PCP (No, not that one, the Primary Control Program!), DOS (Disk Operating System: Yes, there was a DOS before Steve Jobs got out of school!), MFT (Multiprogramming with a Fixed number of Tasks), and MVT (Multiprogramming with a Variable number of Tasks). MVT begat Single Virtual System (SVS), which begat Multiple Virtual System (MVS). We point proudly to the progression of operating systems that are upward compatible based on the IBM System/360, System/370, and System/390 hardware. We have seen programs that ran on the System/360 now run on the System/390 *without having to be recompiled*. The current IBM MVS/ESA, VSE/ESA (from DOS/VSE), and VM/ESA operating systems give us powerful platforms for computing and a wonderful legacy of management tools.

1.1.1 Logical View

In this environment, referred to as the *glass house* (Figure 1-1), IBM has controlled the operating system. Its internal laboratories create different architectures (for example, MVS, VSE, VM, and TPF), but the control has been in the hands of one company.

Figure 1-2 shows one generic picture of the heritage system configuration.

Since the early times, a terminal has connected to the programs via some terminal control program. In the really early days, we wrote our own terminal control programs, but soon the Telecommunications Access

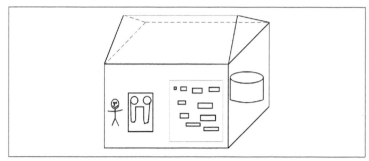

Figure 1-1. Ye Olde Glass House

The mainframe environment is sometimes called the glass house because companies often place all of the consoles and other control mechanisms in a glass-walled room adjacent to the computer room. This way the operators can see the equipment they control yet be isolated from the noise. People have different environmental requirements than mainframe computers!

Method (TCAM), Virtual Telecommunications Access Method (VTAM), and Systems Network Architecture (SNA) protocol made it much simpler to attach terminals to an application. The second copy of MVS at the bottom of the figure shows that it is easy to configure terminals from one application to another. It could be in the same room, within 60 kilometers sharing peripherals such as direct access storage devices (DASDs) and tape or cartridge drives, or networked anywhere in the world.

In the Customer Information Control System (CICS) subsystem, you could have the terminal owning region on one processor complex and the application owning region in another.

1.2 UNIX Genealogy

It may surprise some mainframe people that a powerful system was growing down the street from IBM (well, maybe a very long street) at AT&T Bell Laboratories when IBM started developing the operating system for the System/360. Figure 1-3 shows the progression. Between 1965 (the same year IBM's System/360 was born) and 1969, the *Multiplexed Information and Computing Service*, or *Multics,*

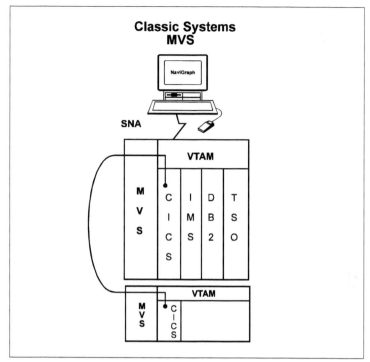

Figure 1-2. Mainframe Configuration

*This view shows two copies of MVS running in two processor
complexes. At the top is the MVS operating system with the Virtual
Telecommunications Access Method (VTAM) controlling the Systems
Network Architecture (SNA) communications protocol for terminal
access to MVS. CICS, the world-class transaction processing
subsystem, uses VTAM and MVS services. IMS, DB2, and other
database subsystems are available under MVS. The Time Sharing
Option (TSO) subsystem allows terminal users to access all data stored
in the MVS environment. Another copy of MVS could be attached
across the room, across the city, or around the world. In this
environment, you can have a single point of control, such as Landmark's
NaviGraph, a PC-based GUI tool.*

operating system was developed by the General
Electric Company, AT&T Bell Labs, and the
Massachusetts Institute of Technology. *Multics* was
developed to allow many users to access a single
computer simultaneously as well as to share their data
and the cost of a computer system. The research to
build Multics was transported to Honeywell GECOS
as a file system handler, and then onto PDP-07

machines. [The evolution of stronger and better file systems in operating systems is not new. The mainframe platform struggled with file system ease-of-use until the Virtual Sequential Access Method (VSAM) was created in the early 1980s.]

Ken Thompson, Dennis Ritchie, Brian Kernighan, and others at Bell Labs worked on a file system that stored data in a way similar to Multics. [They actually wanted an efficient way to store games on a PDP-07! The PDP-07 was borrowed, so they moved the new file system to a PDP-11/20.] UNIX was born in November 1971. It was called the "first edition" after the number assigned to the documentation. This tradition of naming UNIX versions after the documentation has continued. [UNIX is one of the few

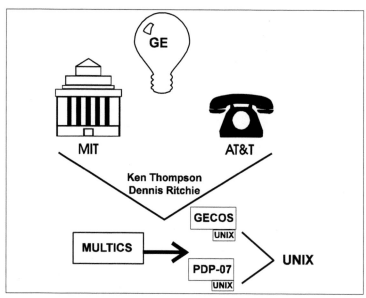

Figure 1-3. UNIX Genealogy

UNIX grew out of the work of a consortium of people at MIT, General Electric, and AT&T on an I/O and development system for the Multics operating system. Eventually, Ken Thompson, Dennis Ritchie, and others expanded the system into the C language and the UNIX operating system.

systems that acknowledges that the documentation has been vital to its success.]

The name, dreamed up by Brian Kernighan, was originally Uniplexed Information and Computing System (UNICS) and later changed to *UNIX*. It was a play on words used for the acronym *Multics*. Thompson created an interpretive language for the new system and called it *B*. The replacement, a better compiler, was (of course) *C*. (I wonder what happened to *A*?)

Then AT&T did a very unusual thing — it rewrote UNIX in the C high-level language. The C language was relatively small so it could be ported and it was rich with functionality, easier to read, easy to learn, and thus crowded out assembler as the language of choice.

Back then, AT&T could not market computer products because of the 1956 consent decree with the federal government. But they could share the UNIX system with educational institutions at no charge. Since no revenue was coming in, AT&T did not want to support UNIX, so they distributed it in source code.

Each site that obtained UNIX could add functions or change the distributed functions by changing the source code, recompiling the program, and linking it into the operating system. Basically, UNIX was a *do-it-yourself* operating system. Universities and other sites had a vested interest in sharing data and programs, so the external interfaces remained relatively constant.

In 1974, Thompson and Ritchie produced an ACM paper (ACM 17,7) describing their system. The first port of UNIX to a really new platform was done in 1976 by Richard Miller at the University of Wollongong (UW), south of Sydney, Australia. The University of Sydney had Version 6 of UNIX on a PDP-11/40, but UW could only afford an Interdata 7/32 (Perkin Elmer). The source port went from tape to disk to system to disk to tape, but the port was accomplished. That would be like running MVS on a PC today! (Whoops, they've done that, too — you can't keep these butterflies down!)

This source-based distribution separated UNIX from the mainframe architecture. IBM distributes source code, but with each release, less source code is available to licensing sites. This process is called movement toward *object code only* (OCO).

Very few MVS sites today change and assemble operating system modules. Most functions are added in *exit* routines. Exits are places in the operating system where a branch is taken to a dummy module (it just returns immediately). Data center personnel (or vendors) only need to supply a replacement module for the exit routine and install it in place of the dummy module. UNIX operating systems must move toward exits or Application Programming Interfaces (APIs) to provide documented interfaces. The reason is as simple as looking at the development of the mainframe: UNIX operating system developers want their customers to move quickly from release to release (to avoid having to support many versions). If there are standard interfaces, customers and the customers' vendors can move from release to release without recoding their low-level programs.

The largest and most widely used exit routines are in the MVS Job Entry Subsystems (JES2 and JES3), which control batch job submission and printed or spooled output. UNIX usually has dedicated, low-cost printers attached to systems so these systems do not need complicated spooling systems.

Historically, the UNIX architecture has supported relatively low-cost, incremental upgrades. Scalability still exists, but as processors and networks become larger and more complex, tighter management and control becomes necessary.

UNIX systems administrators are discovering what mainframe Fortran and COBOL programmers found out a long time ago on the mainframe. Compilers are just programs. The program architect must make decisions on such things as how to initialize counters in a loop. One might decrement the counter, check the value, then do the code in the loop. Another might do the work, decrement the counter, then check the value. Slight differences, yet the program behaves differently under different C compilers.

Some common sense helps here: Settle on one compiler and stay with it until you test and understand a new compiler. Don't jump from one to another without knowing how deep the water is.

1

1.2.1   Logical View

In Figure 1-4, we show the open systems (UNIX) configuration. In the beginning, terminals connected directly to a dedicated UNIX processor. As networking grew, just like the mainframe, the

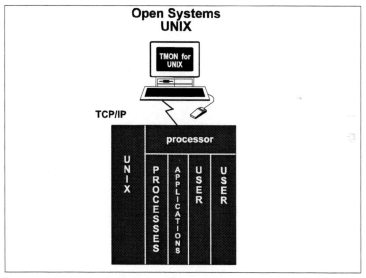

Figure 1-4. Logical UNIX Configuration

UNIX can be shown as an operating system with the TCP/IP networking protocol providing access to UNIX applications. In UNIX, a user logs in (remember, mainframe people would say "logs on") and can run applications. Each task is defined as a process. A single monitor (TMON for UNIX) can monitor one or many of these systems.

operating system supported terminal access to networks through the Transmission Control Protocol/Internet Protocol (TCP/IP).

Figure 1-5 shows a nationwide version of a UNIX environment. This is very similar to what you could do in a mainframe environment, except that each of the nodes could be built with low-cost software and hardware.

The next step is to look at the architecture of these operating systems. You will find that they are really very similar.

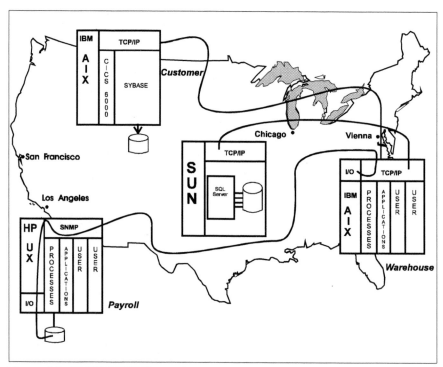

Figure 1-5. UNIX TCP/IP Network

HP, IBM, SCO, and Sun are major distributors of UNIX hardware and software. This figure shows that all of these could be connected in a network to provide access to a wide array of information and applications.

Chapter 2: Architecture

The architecture of MVS is well defined in the System/390 specifications. IBM built the hardware first and then developed the software. You may hear that IBM is a hardware vendor, but much of their business is software. Over the last 30 years, IBM has built upon the OS base until it is a full-function operating system designed for large system data processing. The architecture of UNIX is loosely defined as multiple vendors providing hardware and software.

This publication is not designed to fully discuss the architecture of these two operating systems as that could be the subject of one or more textbook-level publications. (See the list of references in the acknowledgments section of the preface.) It is a comparison of the two architectures and assumes you know a little about one or both of these operating systems.

2.1 Units of Work

A *unit of work* in an operating system is the smallest dispatchable unit. It is usually represented by control blocks maintained by the operating system. The control blocks point to the application code to which the operating system turns over control when it is time to allow applications to access the processor.

2.1.1 Mainframe Task

The primary unit of work in the MVS system is called a *task*. A whole series of control blocks supports the maintenance of the tasks in the system. There may be many tasks housed in a single *address space*. The task may be active (running on a CPU), waiting (in central storage — *in and ready*), or swapped out (to auxiliary storage — *out and ready* or *out and wait*). You will learn more about task status in Chapter 3.

2.1.2   UNIX Process

The unit of work in the UNIX environment is the *process*. Just like the mainframe *task*, this term describes the unique execution of one or more programs by an individual user at a specific point in time. A process also may be referred to as a *daemon*, *kernel*, or *user*. (There are only two industries in the civilized world who call their customers "users." One is the computer industry.)

A *daemon process* is the equivalent to an MVS started task, a disconnected VM service machine, or a PC/DOS terminate and stay resident (TSR) program. I will use the term *daemon process* because that seems to be a complete title. Mainframe people don't say "The MVS JES2 *started* is driving the local and remote printers." They say "The MVS JES2 *STC (started system task) ...*"

Just like a mainframe task, a process may be in one of several states: sleep state, ready state, or swap state. You will learn more about these in the next several chapters.

Table 2-1 compares the basics of these two architectures. For this book, we use the term *task/process* to indicate a unit of work that may be on either platform.

Table 2-1. Mainframe vs. UNIX: Environment

Basic	Mainframe	UNIX
Hardware	IBM Principles of Operation (POP) defines every possible instruction. The original equipment manufacturer's interface (OEMI) provides hardware interface specifications. Some *plug-compatible* vendors provide DASD, control units, and even processors. Any program will run on equivalent hardware from any vendor without recompiling.	Software generally based on UNIX System V is implemented on many different hardware platforms. Hardware at a single location is generally provided by one vendor (for example HP, IBM, or Sun), but each location could have a different vendor. Most programs run on different platforms after recompilation.
Software	Application software is upward compatible without recompilation. New operating system functions are provided by IBM. Other companies provide *applications* extensions (for example, IDMS database or SYNCSORT system sort programs).	The basic UNIX operating system is extended as needed (for example, the Berkeley Software Distribution (BSD)). Programs are portable after recompilation. UNIX shines running turnkey applications.
Primary use	Business applications: accounting, payroll, MIS reporting.	Program development, turnkey systems, department solutions.
Primary unit of work	task	process
Ease-of-use	Relatively difficult to get started. Network must be accessed to use programs or data.	Easy to get started because the architecture is hidden from end user.
How to gain access to the system	*Logon*	*Login*

2

Table 2-1. Mainframe vs. UNIX: Environment		
Basic	**Mainframe**	**UNIX**
Rename a data set	*rename*	*move* (No, there is no rename. Yes, the command really just renames the file and you don't have to have space for both the old and new copy while the command is executing.) Use the -i to force the move command to ask about each rename.

2.2 MVS Architecture

Figure 2-1 shows the mainframe software from the virtual storage viewpoint. MVS/ESA is used as an example, but the System/390 architecture requires the same components for the VM/ESA and VSE/ESA operating systems. The MVS operating system *nucleus* straddles the 16-megabyte line because some of the operating system runs in 24-bit mode (program and data areas are below 16 megabytes and programs can access only the first 16 megabytes) and some in 31-bit mode (run in and access all of two gigabytes). Operating system services are generally accessed by a *supervisor call* operation code.

Access method modules and other shared programs are housed in a common area. Access method modules are generally entered by branch entry and operate in *program mode*.

In MVS, there are two kinds of address spaces in virtual storage. The first is an *executable address space* that contains programs and data intermixed. The operating system and common storage area (at the top and bottom of Figure 2-1) are shared by all address spaces. The second, *data spaces*, are dedicated to data for reference by programs running in executable address spaces.

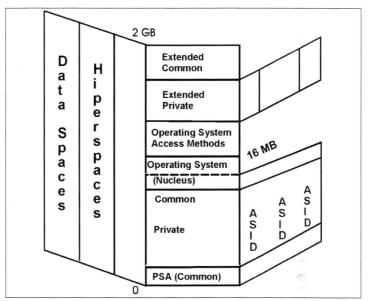

Figure 2-1. MVS/ESA Virtual Storage

In the center of this figure, an MVS/ESA address space is shown with private and operating system areas in the first 16 megabytes. The operating system nucleus straddles the 16-megabyte line (left over from MVS/370 days). Extended areas are between 16 megabyte and the 2-gigabyte line. As additional address spaces are started, they duplicate the private areas and, therefore, are shown as extensions. On the left of the figure are data spaces and hiperspaces that do not have areas for MVS or application modules. The builder of these 2-gigabyte virtual address spaces can put modules or data into the entire two gigabytes.

Hardware-defined communication areas (*prefixed save areas,* or *PSAs*) occupy the first page of storage. Each address space is logically represented as a pop-out box to the 2-gigabyte address space and is identified by an *address space identifier (ASID)* control block. MVS has a table of address space identifiers and the size of the table is set by a parameter (MAXUSER) that can be changed only at IPL time.

The boxes on the left in the figure show that *data spaces* or *hiperspaces* can be two gigabytes big without mapping the common areas in the address space. Thus, all 2-gigabyte spaces can be used to store data or modules.

Figure 2-2 shows the *MVS concentric circle* logical view
of MVS tasks that I have used for decades to show
hardware, operating system, and applications
interactions.

- The System/390 hardware is in the middle ring.
  The operating system is at ring **2**. MVS is used as
  an example but VM, VSE, or even the Transaction
  Processing Facility (TPF) operating system could
  be in control of the hardware. The mainframe
  logical partitioning (LPAR for IBM machines,
  Multiple Domain Facility (MDF) for Amdahl, and
  Multiple Logical Partitions Facility (MLPF) for

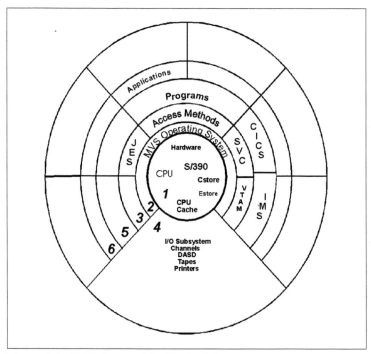

Figure 2-2. MVS Concentric Circles View

*The MVS system is shown here as concentric circles. In the middle is the
hardware. The MVS operating system provides supervisor services.
Application programs and subsystems use the same hardware
instructions as the operating system because an add logical instruction
on one System/390 system operates exactly the same on all System/390
systems (unless the hardware is sick and running a fever!).*

Hitachi) can run all of these operating systems on a single hardware platform at the same time. If *multiprocessing* means having an operating system run on multiple CPUs, is *multioperating* a good term to use for multiple operating systems on more than one CPU?

- Subsystems are shown at ring **3**. These are whole subsystems or just access method modules that provide services to workloads running on the operating system. The first example of a subsystem is the Job Entry Subsystem (JES), which controls startups, logons, batch jobs, and spooled output. For UNIX, this would be the login service, *standard input* and *standard output* functions. Second are access method modules that provide a high-level access to a full-function file subsystem. The third group of services are the *supervisor calls (SVCs)*, which can be used directly by tasks. Branch-entry access also is available to support highly efficient, low-overhead access. The fourth example of services, VTAM, controls terminal and application interfaces between applications.

2

- The hardware is shown at ring **4**. Subsystems and even user-written programs can access hardware directly, but the operating system must be aware of that access to prevent potentially fatal conflicts. It is rare that even *real programmers* access hardware directly.

- At rings **5** and **6**, the transaction processing programs (like CICS, IMS, and IDMS/DC), batch jobs, and TSO users access the operating system and hardware services. These are said to run in *program mode*. On the mainframe, all tasks execute the System/390 instruction set. Tasks can be coded in COBOL, PL/I, or other high-level compiler, but the output object module is machine language. This module can be moved from system to system without compilation. In UNIX, programs are coded in C (or other high-level language) and compiler converts to machine-dependent code. A module compiled on a Sun machine can't be used on an HP machine.

IBM hardware provides *upward-compatible* capabilities. This means subsequent versions of hardware and software support the basic machine instructions. An *add* instruction on the old IBM System/360 Model 50 machines is the same as the add instruction on today's fastest ES/9000 machines. As the hardware progressed from System/360 to System/370 to System/390, additional operation codes (OPCODES) appeared to implement the new functions (such as sorting and encryption). The old stuff always worked.

2.3 UNIX Architecture

Figure 2-3 shows a logical representation of UNIX software and hardware. UNIX hardware is in the center of a circle with the UNIX operating system *kernel* surrounding it. Each hardware platform is unique.

In this representation, customers access UNIX programs and services by entering commands. The commands use standard system calls to access operating system services from the kernel as needed. For example, the file system calls `open`, `read`, `write`, `lseek`, and `close` are used to process the file being edited. These are equivalent to the mainframe access methods services.

Text editors such as `vi` or `emacs` are used for file processing.

In the performance arena, commands such as `iostat` or `sar` access kernel control blocks to gather data. Since each operating system has different control blocks and, therefore, different metrics, the output of these commands is different depending on the version and manufacturer of the software and hardware.

There is no easy way to determine what the metrics mean for the different combinations of software and hardware. You should consult your vendor's documentation and demand that the metrics be fully described. For example, *CPU time* is not acceptable. What is the unit of measure? In MVS, it is milliseconds. In UNIX, it may be timer ticks, seconds, or something else. What is the smallest unit of measurement (for example, 128 microseconds)? What about multiple CPUs? Are there other measurements that may confuse the issue? [The classic case in the MVS environment is the CPU clock used in LPAR environments. The LPAR measures are different from the ones MVS uses and, in many cases, the total operating system numbers do not add up to the LPAR totals.]

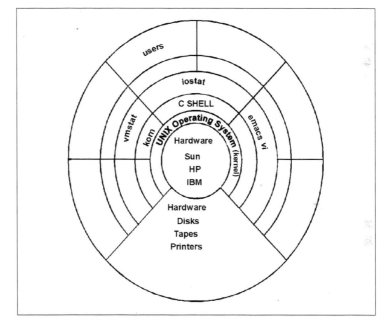

Figure 2-3. UNIX Logical View

UNIX hardware is shown at the center of this view. The operating software surrounds the hardware. Unlike MVS (or VM, VSE, etc.), the operating system software is customized for the hardware. On one hand, that allows applications to be relatively independent of the hardware. Performance monitors and other systems management software are at a great disadvantage. Some (such as Sun/OS) have language extensions to the operating system that make things even more complex. Application programs and subsystems such as database subsystems call operating system routines to get services performed.

2.4 Users and Jobs

TSO sessions in MVS or users in UNIX are the interactive way for people to access these operating systems. Long-running data processing is done by *batch jobs* in MVS and by *batch processes* in UNIX. The operating systems support seldom-ending tasks called *started systems tasks (STCs)* in MVS and *daemon processes* in UNIX.

The maximum number of work units that can run depend on the hardware configuration and workload requirements. In MVS, the *MAXUSER* parameter limits the maximum number of address spaces that can be started. "Users" include system tasks, initiators, and TSO users. You may set the maximum number of users to 300 and actually have 500 tasks running in 300 address spaces! It is confusing, but it makes our jobs more interesting.

UNIX has a similar limit: the *process table size*. This system parameter actually limits the number of processes that can be active, not the number of users or jobs running. As with MVS, a few users can have many more processes running.

Some tasks are created more equal than other tasks. In the mainframe environment, almost any command can be executed from both batch and the interactive TSO environment. Very large, complex processes are best done in batch jobs because a real person is not sitting at a terminal waiting for the transaction to complete. I have seen some whoppers of TSO sessions and CICS transactions. Even under VM, which is a true interactive environment, I have seen math calculations bring processor complexes to their knees.

The same separation should be done in UNIX. Large processes or groups of processes should be placed into a script and run as a background process.

2.5 What? Me Worry about Architecture?

If your first language is mainframe, you probably have struggled with systems management in relatively large, mission-critical applications. Today, you probably are being asked to install, maintain, or connect to more "cost-effective,"[1] open system environments. Your experience with systems management techniques is vital, but you probably don't understand the UNIX *language*.

If you speak open systems most fluently, you probably know enough to get the job done, but may be getting pressure to manage resources better or more fully predict and justify upgrades.

To make matters worse, none of us likes to plan for, or think about, the rough times. Mainframe sites are reluctant to look at distributed, open system architectures. Open system sites must implement the systems management disciplines taken for granted in the mainframe world to support mission-critical applications.

2

It is vital that we help each other, because large or small, the CPU, memory, and I/O devices that are providing acceptable performance today will become bogged down tomorrow. Count on that!

2.6 Summary

Table 2-2 compares the architectural components of the two operating systems.

---

1   Most evaluations now show that distributed and desktop cost-per-seat over a 5-year period are about one and one-half times the cost of mainframe solutions.

Table 2-2. Mainframe vs. UNIX: Components		
Grouping	**Mainframe**	**UNIX**
Operating system	MVS/ESA, VM/ESA, or VSE/ESA *nucleus*.	*System kernel* or just *kernel*.
Access to supervisor services	*Supervisor call (SVC)* for MVS and VSE. 256 are defined, but several (for example, SVC router: 109) serve as multiple calls. SVCs run in *privileged mode*. Newer services use the *PC Call* facility. VM uses *diagnose* calls similar to SVCs. MVS also provides branch entry access for privileged programs, which provides for fast access without having to wait for redispatch.	Calls to system service routines.
Executable files	Programs in load libraries.	Executable file.
Control unit of work	Job step or TSO address space with one or more *task control blocks (TCBs)*.	*Process*.
Table of tasks/processes	ASID list of dispatchable ASIDs.	Process table.
Command interpreter	*Time Sharing Option (TSO)*.	*Shell*
Asynchronous work	*Batch processing*.	*Background commands. (using the "&" parameter on commands)*.
Common storage place for popular or distributed commands or programs	*SYS1.LINKLIB*.	*/bin* directory.
Branch to start a task	*ATTACH* macro creates a *subtask*.	*exec* system call.
Start additional work	*ATTACH* macro creates a *subtask*.	*fork* system call creates a *child* process.
Wait for work to be done	*WAIT* macro.	*wait* system call.

Table 2-2. Mainframe vs. UNIX: Components

Grouping	Mainframe	UNIX
Complete task	*Exit: SVC 3* or branch to register 14 contents at entry.	*exit* system call.
Transfer control to a new task	*XCTL.*	*execl* system call.
Case sensitivity	MVS JCL requires uppercase letters only.	UNIX commands are very case sensitive. Generally, use lowercase letters and do not mix case.

2

Part II: CPU, Storage, and I/O

The second part of this book considers the three components of computing you should understand to make sound decisions concerning problems and potential problems in your computing environment. The MVS and UNIX platforms are compared side by side. I think you will see that the two have similar components. The reason is simple: All computing systems must have a minimum set of components to be able to provide services to applications running under the operating system.

The first component, discussed in Chapter 3, is the central processing unit (CPU), which is the part of the computer that implements the instructions of the platform to add, subtract, move, and compare data. Every computer has a definite number of instructions and each instruction operates in a specific manner.

The second component of the computer, discussed in Chapter 4, is central storage (also called real storage, core storage, main storage, or processor complex storage). This is the part of the computer that contains instructions and data.

The final component, discussed in Chapter 5, is the I/O subsystem. Most studies show that 80% of all performance problems are I/O related. It stands to reason that this, and chapter 7, may be the most important chapters in the book.

Capture Ratio

Smart readers read all of the words and here is the tip buried for you to find. We look at systems through the eyes of monitors. Systems monitors, database monitors, application monitors. It may surprise you to know that what you see is not always what is actually happening. Not all CPU usage is included in the CPU statistics. Not all I/O operations are counted.

In the mainframe world, we refer to this as the concept of *capture ratio*. In the early days of IBM operating systems, it was not unusual to find the operating system reporting only 50% of the CPU being used. We even said, "The CPU is saturated when it gets to 50%!" Some of us used hardware monitors to get the real utilization and compared it to the reported values. Guess where the rest went? To the operating system itself, acting on behalf of the running tasks (for example, I/O operations or storage maintenance)! Today, MVS is one of the most successful in the world at accurately capturing the task doing its work. MVS typically captures or assigns usage in the 80% range.

Performance monitors and the act of monitoring itself use up resources and distort the measurements. Many monitors can use 5%, 15%, up to almost any amount of resource just *measuring* the environment.

Don't let that fool you. Many tasks absorb CPU and may or may not be trackable. Some mainframe monitors, using cross-memory services, spread out their resource usage so it is hard to spot what is being spent. Some mainframe components (like the media manager in MVS) even stop counting. Insist on systems that do their work in address spaces MVS can monitor. But, MVS is not wholly blameless. Even mainframe LPAR management loses some of the time it spends managing resources.

So where does that leave us with UNIX? The answer is that there also IS a capture ratio for UNIX, the industry just has not quantified it. Not all CPU is being captured. One of the causes may be rounding problems. When using the application programming interface (API) to record process CPU utilization, we see some versions of HP/UX *truncating* CPU time to the next lowest second. Thus if you have many processes that use less than 1 second CPU time, you may be capturing much less CPU than actually being used. A way around this is to use the accounting records to verify your process data. As of this writing, some IBM AIX data fields are wrong. I don't know about SUN or other systems.

Not all I/Os are being recorded. Not all storage is being reported. What percent is missing? I don't know and probably no one else knows either. Just remember that you won't get 100% of your computing resources. Not because it is not being used and used productively, but because the tools are not honed yet.

Another area not to be fooled by is having system accounting active. In MVS, the RMF (or CMF) subsystem is used to capture data. Few MVS sites run without SMF. In the UNIX world, the `accton` command starts up accounting needed for many of the performance monitors. Most sites run without `accton`. If you turn accounting on, you will lose a percentage of your resources, but you may be able to solve a problem with the information you gather. The only other option is to install a performance monitor like **The Monitor** for UNIX by Landmark Systems to gather the data. [**The Monitor** for UNIX has become a component of Landmark's *PerformanceWorks* product line, which includes operating system, database, and framework integration.]

Finally, UNIX systems have a propensity to loose track of processes. These are called *orphan* processes. One example under AIX 4.1.4 was the AMD command to gather statistics for NFS mounted files. It spauned a process to gather the information. Unfortunately, the process sometimes did not go away. Even the command did not get rid of the process. These orphan processes may or may not be using resources that you can identify.

The bad news is that you must manage the data from that monitor and keep that data for reference just like MVS systems folks have to do with SMF.

The penalty for not having systems management tools in place is that you must throw money at problems, not knowing if the money helps or hurts your goals.

II

Chapter 3: CPU Utilization Management

I discuss the CPU first because it is the easiest and
most important resource to manage. Total control
over CPU allocation is possible on the mainframe
(especially under MVS). In the client/server, open
systems world, managing CPU resource is just
beginning to take on the importance it has had in the
mainframe world for years. The reason is simple: On
the mainframe, the CPU is a very expensive and
limited resource. We manage it because we must.

In the UNIX world, CPU resources are cheaper and
more readily available. It is easy to see, from price
lists, that adding MIPS to a UNIX system is cheaper
than adding MIPS to a mainframe. *[MIPS (millions of
instructions per second) is an acronym indicating the
power of a processor, sometimes referred to as
meaningless indicator of processor service.]* Problems
crop up when you are out of CPU and can't add more
without an expensive upgrade. As UNIX processors
become more powerful, management of them
becomes more vital. Sooner or later, even UNIX
systems administrators will have to manage the CPU
resource.

Wouldn't it be better to learn now how to keep your
ox out of the ditch instead of going into panic mode
later when both the ox and cart end up there?

3.1 What Does a CPU Do?

A *program* is a series of instructions developed to
accomplish a specific task. The program can be as
complicated as a payroll application or as simple as a
program *routine* that adds all the values in a row from
a table. Each of these instructions is *executed* by the
CPU, one at a time, until the program ends or *branches*
to another program. The key concept is that a CPU
accomplishes work, one instruction at a time.

The possible instructions a CPU can work with are
outlined in a manual specific to the machine's

3

architecture. For example, in the IBM mainframe world, IBM's *Principles of Operation (POP)* contains all the instructions and what they can do. Programmers like a system with a big menu of instructions, because they can select just the right one for the problem at hand.

The mainframe is the real open architecture. The Original Equipment Manufacturer's Interface (OEMI) specifications state how to build CPU, DASD, tape, and other mainframe components. Several manufacturers provide CPUs and many manufacturers provide peripherals for mainframe operation.

UNIX hardware is delivered as a turnkey environment of hardware and software. You buy HP from Hewlett Packard, IBM from IBM, and Sun from Sun. Each has its own instruction set and interfaces.

The IBM System/390 is a *complex instruction set computer (CISC)*. It has a large number of instructions and several instruction sizes.

Recently, another concept, *reduced instruction set computers (RISCs)*, has developed. RISCs are purported to be faster and more efficient because they limit the number and types of instructions available to the programmer. Think of RISC as the fast-food version of computers. One of the things that made McDonald's successful around the world is that you can have anything you want as long as it looks like a hamburger, fries, and a soft drink. (True, today they are expanding into other areas, but their corporate strategy really is fast, efficient, cost-effective meals for families.)

This philosophy should be used by the corporate data center. The motto should be that the data center will provide fast, efficient, cost-effective data processing whether it is a full-course meal (MVS), department-sized, turnkey applications (UNIX), or personal solutions (personal computers or laptops).

Don't get caught in a rut like the railroads did. If the railroad industry had realized they were in the *transportation* business instead of just the *railroad* business, you would be flying on airplanes with names such as Norfolk and Southern or Santa Fe! Mainframe users should realize that complementary metal oxide semiconductor (CMOS) CPU power is much cheaper than mainframe CPU. Companies buy cheap stuff. UNIX readers, don't neglect systems management disciplines. Chief executive officers (CEOs) and chief financial officers (CFOs) won't let you endanger the company's data and your customers' data processing.

In any case, the CPU is a valuable resource that is available to process instructions. To manage that resource successfully, you need to know something about the CPU.

3.2 Who Is Using the CPU?

The first question to ask when looking at a system's CPU utilization is "Who is using the CPU?" Historically on the mainframe, we determine peak usage hours (for example, 10-11 a.m. and 2-3 p.m.), build a database to track usage by account and user, and project the growth or decline rate. We can see what the utilization was and is, and where it is going.

One of the things I would change in most UNIX performance monitoring would be to concentrate on the peaks instead of looking at daily averages. Just as I do in some mainframe environments, I often see performance specialists monitoring a 10-hour average. That seems useless to me. How do you distinguish between a narrow period of overload and a broad period of moderate business? What if people and tasks were delayed from 10 a.m. to 11 a.m., and your customers were mad, but your daily averages only went up a few points?

The hard part is determining which workload is causing the changes and deciding what to do about it.

3

The operating system switches tasks/processes at machine speed. You need detailed data to allocate usage to the proper task/process.

What happens when the operating system dispatches a task/process? Figure 3-1 shows a UNIX kernel (MVS supervisor) running at ①. When the kernel dispatches a process at ②, the process continues to run until it issues a syscall (SVC in MVS) or gets interrupted. At that time, a higher priority process (task in MVS) might be dispatched at ③. User #1 is ready to run but is delayed because User #2 has a higher priority. User #2, at ③, continues until it issues a syscall or an interrupt occurs.

3.2.1 Multitask Creation

In MVS and VSE environments, the operating system *attach* function gives the program the ability to have two tasks available to run on the CPU. Multitasking is

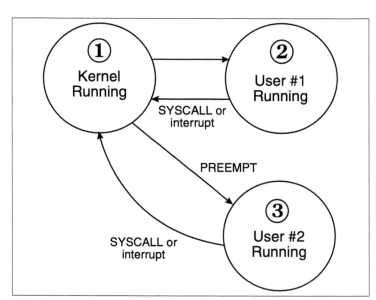

Figure 3-1. Giving Up CPU

At ①, the UNIX kernel calls a user, program, or process to turn control of the CPU over to that entity. At ②, that entity relinquishes control voluntarily (syscall) or involuntarily (interrupt). If the interrupt was for User #2, then User #1 is said to be preempted.

used for two reasons. The first is to overlap I/O operations. I/O service times are hundreds of times slower than CPU instruction times and will forever be so. Having more than one task to use CPU makes the best use of resources. The second reason for multitasking is to minimize the cost of computing. If a single task/process takes 10 minutes and no other task/process is sharing the resources, the cost of the entire processor complex is born by a single unit of work.

Figure 3-2 shows how UNIX creates a second process — a process called *forking*. MVS uses the term *subtasking*. One of the UNIX system calls is the fork command. That command returns to the UNIX kernel and a second process is created (at ③).

Both processes are ready to run. The operating system selects the one with the highest dispatching priority, not necessarily the highest number. Without

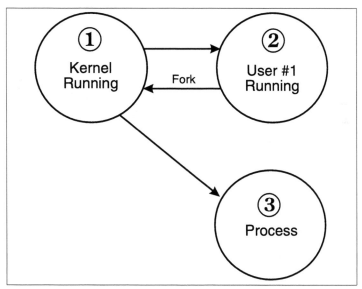

Figure 3-2. Creating Additional Processes

One thing a task/process may want to do is to create another thread (subtask). In UNIX, the creation process is called forking. A kernel syscall is used and another process is started. At ③, the new process is started and competes for system resources.

some balancing technique, User #1 could wait until the requested process is completely done before getting control back. That scenario may be OK or it may not be OK, depending on how important User #1 is.

3.3 Interrupts

As the operating system dispatches tasks/processes, either each task/process gives up control of the CPU voluntarily or the CPU is taken away from it. The interrupt process is an architectural requirement for all hardware/software combinations.

Table 3-1 displays the types of interrupts in each platform, in descending order of importance. The first row has priority over the subsequent rows. In other words, if a machine check interrupt is pending at the same time a DASD device is ready, the machine check is processed first. This makes sense. If the *add* instruction is not working, it is useless to try to add one to the count of I/O operations!

Note that the UNIX system provides for three levels of priority for I/O devices. Network devices are at a higher priority than terminals. This is different from System/390 as it generally allows first-come-first-served access to the processor.

Table 3-1. Interrupts		
Interrupt	**Mainframe**	**UNIX**
Machine errors	Machine check	Machine errors
Clock and time of day	Time of day	Clock
I/O devices	Any I/O device	Disk
		Network devices
		Terminals
Software interrupts	Program check	Software interrupts
	Supervisor call	

The software enables or disables each type of interrupt by setting a special register (called the *program status word (PSW)* in System/390).

The status of the running task/process is saved until after the interrupt is processed. Mainframe address space control blocks (ASCBs) hold information about the interrupted task. Machine check interrupts are always the most important. If the add instruction is not working, it is useless to continue.

3.4 Task/Process States

Both systems have tasks/processes in various states. Figure 3-3 shows the MVS version of state processing. This figure shows three columns, or *states*. The column on the left is the application program running in *program mode*. At ①, the program issues an OPEN macro. Since this is a COBOL program, it branches into the run-time modules. At ②, the run-time module issues an SVC. This is the first real state change and is required because the MVS operating system must perform work (such as getting buffer areas in common, protected storage). At ③, the supervisor sets the run mode back to program and branches back to the run-time module, which returns to the application program (at ④). Later in the program, maybe just nanoseconds (at ⑤), the program issues a read macro to access one of the logical records. The record is moved from the physical buffer to the application buffer area (assuming *get move* access).

3

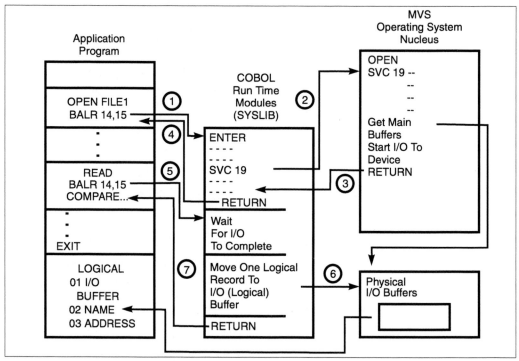

Figure 3-3. MVS State Processing

Most computer systems, like MVS pictured here, have three major segments of resource usage. On the left, application programs issue high-level calls (open), which usually branch into run-time, or access method, modules. These modules call supervisor services to complete the requested action.

Figure 3-4 shows the same process, only this time the hardware is included. Note that on either mainframe or UNIX, if one and only one task/process is running, only the speed of the peripheral device meters how long the I/O operation delayed the application. If multiple tasks are running, delays can take place if the other tasks are accessing the same device or other devices on the same path.

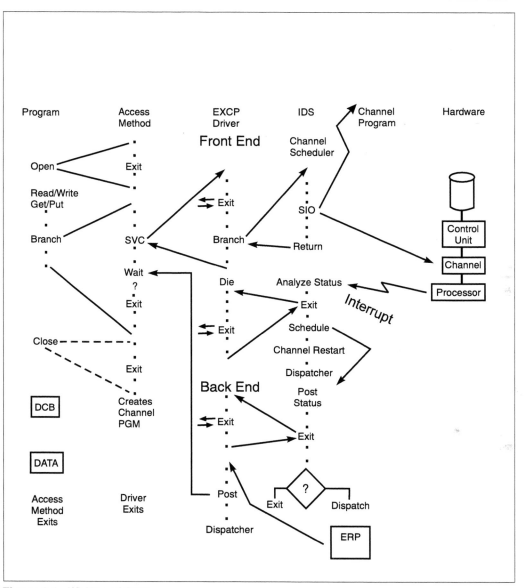

Figure 3-4. I/O Use of CPU

A more detailed diagram of CPU usage when an application requests an I/O operation is shown here. Do not try to understand each of the components because the explanation of this figure could take a chapter! Just visualize the flow: The same program and access method is on the left. The operating system components (EXCP I/O driver) and the Input/Output Supervisor (IOS) are shown on the right. In System/390 systems, the I/O operation rarely steals CPU cycles from executing. programs. In some UNIX hardware configurations, the I/O operation may steal CPU cycles from the application.

Table 3-2 lists the states in which a task/process can exist.

Table 3-2. Descriptions of Task/Process States	
State	**Description**
Running	The task/process has control of the CPU and is executing instructions.
Waiting for I/O	The task/process has asked for a file read, write, or position on a device.
Waiting for supervisor services	The task/process has asked for some supervisor service such as get storage or ask for the time of day. Technically, this is an extension of the instructions for the task/process. Since it is not the actual program, the operating system may count the time spent in a different timer. In MVS, this is supervisor request block (SRB) time. In UNIX, it is SY, or system kernel servicing, time.
Preempted	The task has been suspended by a task with a higher priority. Usually this takes place if the running task asks for a supervisor service or an I/O operation, or a very short timer interval has expired.
Waiting in storage	If the task/process is waiting for some event such as the terminal to respond, it may be *logically swapped in* (mainframe) or asleep in memory (UNIX). If memory is needed, the task can be moved to auxiliary storage.
Waiting but out of main memory	In the MVS environment, this is *physically swapped out*; in UNIX, it is *sleep, swapped*.

3.5 Dispatching Priorities

Both the mainframe and UNIX platforms use *round robin, prioritized* dispatching schedulers and a single number from zero to 255 to indicate dispatching priority. In the round robin method, a list of tasks/processes is maintained in some order. The

most important task/process that is ready is
dispatched, meaning that control of the CPU is turned
over to the task/process. This task/process continues
to execute instructions until it gives up control (SVC
or system call) or some external event interrupts.

Both mainframe and UNIX systems provide for
dispatching priority changes either by the system or
by the application itself. The mainframe uses the
CHAP macro/service (although privileged tasks can
directly change the priority). UNIX uses the `nice`
command to alter priorities.

3.5.1   Mainframe Dispatching Priorities

OS/390 (the mainframe) in general, and the MVS
implementation speicifically, has the most detailed
and flexible control for dispatching tasks of any
operating system. This section describes in depth
what I believe is required for complete control. It
describes all versions of MVS before OS/390 and
OS/390 operating in compatability mode. Even in
goal mode, SRM is alive and well, only these numbers
are manipulated by the workload manager.

3.5.1.1   A Look at the Numbers

Table 3-3 shows MVS dispatching priorities. Each
block of 16 numbers is assigned to an automatic
priority group range (APGRNG).

Table 3-3. MVS Dispatching Priorities			
Hex	**Decimal**	**APGRNG**	**Set**
F0-FF	240-255	15	9
E0-EF	224-239	14	8
D0-DF	208-223	13	7
C0-CF	192-207	12	6
B0-BF	176-191	11	5
A0-AF	160-175	10	4

3

Table 3-3. MVS Dispatching Priorities			
Hex	**Decimal**	**APGRNG**	**Set**
90-9F	144-159	9	3
80-8F	128-143	8	2
70-7F	112-127	7	1
60-6F	96-111	6	0

A large number of changes have been made to the MVS dispatcher over the years to capitalize on multiprocessors and environments. This discussion is general in scope. If you are interested in the specifics of a particular version of MVS, you probably need to run GTF traces to determine exactly how the dispatcher on your system is running as it changes from release to release and machine to machine!

MVS arranges address spaces in two queues. The first queue contains *dispatchable address spaces*, or ASIDs available for processing. The second queue contains *nondispatchable address spaces*, or ASIDs not available for processing. In both cases, the ASIDs are arranged in descending dispatching priority. Dispatching priority is a number from 0 to 255, or x'00' to x'FF'. The higher the dispatching priority, the more likely the address space will get to use the CPU.

Later MVS dispatchers even subdivide dispatchable address spaces with a *ready queue* and a *true ready queue*.

3.5.1.2   Setting MVS Dispatching Priorities

For non-goal mode MVS, the data center specifies the performance group for tasks either specifically (using a fully qualified name such as PAYROLL1) or generically (using a name such as PAY starting in position 1) in SYS1.PARMLIB(IEAICSxx).

In SYS1.PARMLIB(IEAIPSxx), performance group dispatching priorities are assigned using the keyword DP=txy. These parameters are described in Table 3.4.

Table 3-4. Value of DP=txy	
Parameter	**Description**
t	The type of priority. Valid values are: **F** (fixed), which assigns a dispatching priority that does not change over time. **R** (rotate), which assigns several address spaces the same dispatching priority. MVS rotated the address space so each one had some percentage at the top of the single priority number. I use the past tense because rotate was eliminated in MVS releases beginning with 3.x, but it pops up in other operating systems so I keep it here to show MVS had it. **M** (mean-time-to-wait), which assigns the top priority in a group (for example, 149 in the range of 140 to 149) for the first time slice a task gets and then adjusts up or down based on the task giving up control of the CPU voluntarily.
x	The APG set. Valid values are any number from 0 through 15 that subdivides the 256 priority numbers into 16 groups.
y	The position in the fixed queue. Specify this parameter only if $t = F$. Valid values are any number from 1 through 5.

I recommend mean-time-to-wait (MTW) for almost all important workloads. MTW was developed by the original HASP programmers. [Houston Automated Spooler Program was a predecessor to JES2 for the System/360 operating environment]. They noticed that if one region (in the operating system, a *region* was the equivalent to today's *address space*) had a dispatching priority higher than other regions and used a large amount of CPU time, the other regions could not get very good throughput. By rotating the dispatch priority based on the following, throughput could be substantially increased.

- An MVS timer service (STIMER) was set for some number of milliseconds — 200, for example.

3

- A region was dispatched. If the region did not voluntarily give up control by the time the STIMER expired, the region was said to be *CPU bound*, and the dispatching priority would be lowered by some value.

- If the region voluntarily gave up control before the time slice expired, the region was said to be *I/O bound*, and the dispatching priority would be raised by some value.

For example, let's look at APGRNG 15 in Table 3-5 and apply each of the three types of priorities.

- **Fixed**. If *DP=F90* is specified, the address space would always run in dispatching priority 251, or x'FB'. If a unit of work is assigned to F91, it always will be dispatched before a unit of work assigned F90. If two or more units of work are assigned the same number, the first one started will be dispatched first.

- **Rotate**. If *DP=R9* is coded, the address spaces would always be at the same dispatching priority — 250, or x'FA' — but MVS would rotate their position on the queue with others in R9 so that each got a share of the resources. Some data centers use rotate with CICS or other database address spaces. Each address space gets a time slice at the top of the queue. (Remember: Rotate was eliminated in MVS/ESA because it used too many resources (CPU time) and did not really work.)

- **MTW**. Units of work that give up control of the CPU voluntarily (system call or wait) are at the top (that is, M9) and those in a CPU loop are at the bottom (that is, F0). If *DP=M9* were specified, the dispatching priority would vary from 240 to 249. MVS would look at the average time an address space waited and raise the number if it had waited some time and lower the number if it were "hogging" the resource. I have been very successful specifying that CICS address spaces be in a mean-time-to-wait group.

Table 3-5. APGRNG 15 Priorities			
Hex	**Decimal**	**DP=txy**	**Type**
FF	255	F94	Fixed
FE	254	F93	Fixed
FD	253	F92	Fixed
FC	252	F91	Fixed
FB	251	F90	Fixed
FA	250	R9	Rotate
F9	249	M9	MTW
F8	248	M9	MTW
F7	247	M9	MTW
F6	246	M9	MTW
F5	245	M9	MTW
F4	244	M9	MTW
F3	243	M9	MTW
F2	242	M9	MTW
F1	241	M9	MTW
F0	240	M9	MTW

3.5.1.3 Special Dispatching Priorities

Table 3-6 shows some "special" dispatching priorities. If the address space is in virtual storage and available for execution, the dispatching priority is a value from x'02' through x'FE'. If the address space is *logically swapped*, MVS sets the dispatching priority to x'01'.

3

Table 3-6. MVS Dispatching and Swapping

Where	Who	Dispatch Priority
In storage	ASID 10 ASID 20	02-FE 02-FE
Logically swapped	ASID 30	01
Physically swapped out	ASID 40 ASID 50	FF FF

MVS dispatching priorities also tell something about where the task is located.

- If the address is in storage (as ASID 10 and 20 are), their dispatching priority is between 02 and FE (or FF if you have assigned the absolute highest priority. FF is usually reserved for MVS address spaces.)

- If the address space is logically swapped, the dispatching priority is 01. The term *logically swapped* is used for address spaces that have been placed in a wait (for example, waiting for a terminal to respond). It is likely that the address space will become active shortly, so MVS places the address space on a queue that remains in real storage but is not on the active queue. In Table 3-6, ASID 30 is logically swapped out.

- If the address space is physically swapped, the dispatching priority is FF. (Remember: A physically swapped address space can't be dispatched. It must be brought into storage first.) If the address space is physically swapped out and not available for dispatch, the dispatching priority is set to x'FF'. Some MVS address spaces are set to dispatching priority x'FF' to be the highest task in the system. Most of these address spaces are *nonswappable* — so important to MVS that the system resources manager (SRM) will not or cannot swap them out.

3.5.2   UNIX Dispatching Priorities

There are two important numbers UNIX uses in dispatching processes. The first is the *current*, or *actual, execution priority*. UNIX platforms use a wide range of valid numbers. In all cases, the first dispatched user has the lowest number, zero being the *highest priority*. Many platforms use an integer between zero and 127. In the case of AIX Version 3, the values range from zero (high) to 40 (low).

The second important number is the UNIX `nice` number, which may be a value from 0 (which makes the process higher in the priority scheme) to 39 (which makes the process lower in the priority scheme). UNIX supports the `nice` command (and system call), and some versions support the `renice` command.

Before UNIX System V Release 4, dispatching priorities were quite variable. With Release 4, UNIX implemented a *class structure* that defines three priority classes and an array of priorities for each class.

Real-time class processes use a fixed-priority scheduling policy that remains fixed until the user changes them. A real-time process can literally take over the processor.

System-class processes use a fixed priority policy. These are reserved for the kernel and include services such as pageout and scheduling. From the MVS viewpoint, this is like having end users above the master address space. A curious implementation.

Time-shared class processes are the default for UNIX processes and are similar to what UNIX had before Release 4. The objective is to give a fair share of CPU time to each process. It is most like the mainframe mean-time-to-wait priority in that it adapts to the process's operating characteristics.

Table 3-7 gives an overview of these classes.

3

Table 3-7. UNIX Dispatching and Swapping		
Priority Class	**Scheduling Sequence**	**Global Value**
Real time	first	159 . . 100
System	second	60 . . 99
Time-shared	last	59 . . 0

3.6 Multiprogramming and Multiprocessing

One of the most confusing computer principles concerns the amount of work that can be done simultaneously. I'm constantly amazed that some industry writers get the terms jumbled. It's really no wonder, because everyone assumes they know what the terms mean and then they interchange them! I've found the following terms used (there may be more): multitasking, multiprocessing, simultaneous execution, simultaneous processing, multiprogramming, concurrent processing, tightly coupled multiprocessing, loosely coupled multiprocessing, massively parallel processing, parallel sysplex, asymmetric multiprocessing, and symmetric multiprocessing.

I think you could combine all of these into two categories: *multiprogramming*, in which two or more programs share the resources available in a processor complex (which has one or more CPUs, shared storage, and shared I/O facilities) and *multiprocessing*, in which you have two or more central processor units that execute computer instructions simultaneously.

3.6.1   Multiprogramming

The term *multiprogramming* is used wherever you have instructions from one program interleaved with instructions from another program in the same processor complex. On the mainframe, it is also called *multitasking* because there are multiple task control blocks (TCBs) available that point to programs waiting to execute.

Almost all general-purpose computers today have multiprogramming capabilities. In the PC world, you might have a printer driver sending material to an attached printer while you are working on the next letter, memorandum, or spreadsheet. In the UNIX or distributed world, you have users editing scripts and databases processing queries.

On the mainframe, *multiprogramming* implies that the operating system can handle tasks in a queue ready for execution. This term refers to the software architectural design: Can it support two or more units of work at the same time? Each unit of work can be anywhere on the continuum of its processing.

Note: **If there is only one CPU in the box, only one task runs while all other tasks wait.**

The software switches from task to task by interrupting the process and turning control over to another task for a while. This might mean several CICS, IMS, or DB2 environments handling the requests from thousands of users. The term *loosely coupled multiprocessing* is confusing because it describes two processor complexes that can accept work; therefore, it is multiprocessing. But once the work is moved onto one copy of MVS, it can't use the resources of the other copy, so it is really an extension of multiprogramming! Confused yet?

Today's modern operating systems implement multiprogramming by turning control over to each task/process for a predetermined amount of time called a *time slice*. The task/process can give up

3

control voluntarily or involuntarily back to the operating system.

3.6.2   Multiprocessing

Multiprocessing only exists where there are two or more CPUs available to each program to execute program instructions. You also might see the terms *simultaneous execution, simultaneous processing, concurrent processing, tightly coupled multiprocessing, massively parallel processing, parallel sysplex,* and *symmetric multiprocessing* in place of multiprocessing.

For example, I've seen *simultaneous processing* used without regard to the hardware configuration. I have even seen the term used when the author clearly understood that he was discussing single-CPU hardware!

Simultaneous implies that one task is performing machine instructions at the exact same nanosecond that another task is performing instructions. That feat requires multiple CPUs in the box and an operating system that can handle the configuration.

Multiprocessing implies that a single processor complex can handle two or more tasks executing instructions at the same instant. The processor complex must have more than one hardware CPU to process instructions; the software must have the capability to dispatch one instruction in each CPU.

Multiprocessing is a far more complex implementation to deal with from an operating system viewpoint. Queuing and locking mechanisms must be used to protect data and instructions. The most common problem that pops up when you move to true multiprocessing is intermittent dumps that occur during busy time. The reason they occur is that some system service did not obtain the correct lock and overlaid a common area. One of the tasks/processes (and maybe the whole system) abends.

Multiprocessing is much better for multitasking environments because, on a single-CPU machine, if one task is highest in dispatching priority and is hogging the CPU, all tasks below it are locked out and never execute until it finishes or gives up control.

That concept is true for the largest mainframe running MVS/ESA as well as the smallest platform running UNIX. It is more significant, however, on the smaller, single-CPU platform — where one process can block the entire system — than on a large 6-CPU mainframe where it takes six inconsiderate tasks to mess things up.

3.6.3   MVS Multiprocessing

As explained earlier, multiprocessing adds a whole new set of considerations to operating system design. MVS grew up with, and now almost demands, multiple CPUs for efficient operation. The number of CPUs is most efficient when the number is low (for example, two to four CPUs), but MVS can operate very nicely with a 10-CPU setup. Thus, we will assume MVS handles multiprocessing very efficiently up to a point (say, 10 CPUs).

Figure 3-5 shows the two types of mainframe multiprocessing environments.

The first mainframe multiprocessing environment is *tightly coupled multiprocessing,* where multiple CPUs are inside a single box and the MVS control program dispatches tasks as they become ready, on one of the CPUs. The bottom half of the figure shows the other environment, called *loosely coupled multiprocessing,* where more than one copy of MVS controls the same number of processor complexes and they share workload on a DASD spool volume. There are two implementations of this configuration: JES2 and JES3. MVS is moving toward a combination of these subsystems.

3

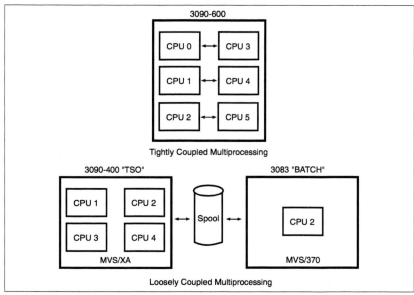

Figure 3-5. MVS Multiprocessing

MVS implements two types of multiprocessing. The first type, tightly coupled multiprocessing, dispatches a unit of work in a processor complex that has all CPUs inside a physical box (or on a single card!). The second type, loosely coupled multiprocessing, has separate copies of MVS in two or more processor complexes. Communication (and, therefore, dispatching) is performed by some communication medium such as DASD.

3.6.4   UNIX Multiprocessing

UNIX was designed and grew up with only one CPU in mind, which would indicate only multiprogramming is possible. The different implementations of UNIX, however, also allow multiprocessing. Some of the implementations are presented here.

3.6.4.1   Asymmetric and Symmetric Multiprocessing

Just like the mainframe, having more than one CPU in a box allows the UNIX operating system to run more than one process concurrently. *Asymmetric multiprocessing* means that a process is dedicated to a single CPU in the box. This is similar to OS/390 parallel sysplex in that there are multiple servers

(CPUs), but once you get into a line, you can't jump over to another CPU to get your instructions executed.

Symmetric multiprocessing is more like the mainframe tightly coupled multiprocessing. Any process can be dispatched on any CPU when the process is ready to run.

In both cases, processor storage and peripherals are shared among the running processes.

3.6.4.2   Satellite Systems

Figure 3-6 shows the *satellite processor configuration*, which allows the kernel to offload processing to other processors. The other processors do not have

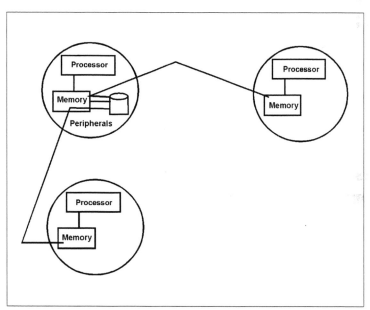

Figure 3-6. UNIX Satellite Processor Configuration

UNIX also can have multiprocessing. In this situation, the CPU and memory of multiple hardware components are used to process applications. Peripherals are used only on the home machine. If these were inside the same physical box, they would be similar to the mainframe attached processor (AP) configurations (no longer offered) or mainframe tightly coupled multiprocessing (except processor memory is not shared).

3

peripherals such as DASD or tape drives. The controlling kernel downloads a special operating system to the satellite configured to pass system calls back to the controlling system. Only the file system and sharing calls are passed back and forth. This is similar to the MVS tightly coupled multiprocessing, except that memory is not shared between the systems.

The benefit of this configuration is that more than one CPU can be completing instructions. I/O operations are the bottleneck, though. All open, close, read, and write operations are passed to the controlling, or *stub*, process.

3.6.4.3   Newcastle Distributed Systems

Figure 3-7 shows the *Newcastle*, or truly distributed, environment. The Newcastle connection is similar to the MVS loosely coupled processing systems. Remote files are flagged as being on another processor and access to them is converted into a remote call.

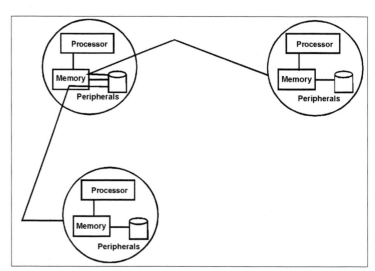

Figure 3-7. True, or Newcastle, Distributed Systems

Note that each system has I/O peripherals, shown here as DASD devices.

It clearly is an attempt to minimize the overhead of passing all operations to the stub process. Only the shared files would have to be delayed by machine-to-machine transfer.

The drawback to this configuration is that all machines must support peripherals for DASD and/or tape access. In other words, it is more management, but less overhead (a lot like life!).

3.6.4.4   Fully Transparent Distributed Systems

Fully transparent distributed systems allow standard path names for files. The kernel recognizes that they are remote and handles the remote call automatically.

3.7   Monitoring CPU Utilization

How do you look at CPU utilization? In the mainframe environment (VM, VSE, or MVS), there are established metrics and methods to capture and report on CPU utilization. For example, Landmark's **The Monitor** for MVS displays and logs CPU utilization.

There are a number of ways to look at CPU utilization with UNIX commands such as vmstat, iostat, and sar. Figure 3-8 shows **The Monitor** for UNIX's CPU Activity by Process report. In this case, *dataserver (23719)* is a Sybase process using 57% of the processor. Is that bad? Maybe. Is that good? Maybe. This particular machine is a test bed running benchmark programs. It is obvious that Sybase is dominating the CPU resource. Only after you look at what is being done by Sybase on behalf of users would you be able to say this is good or bad.

3

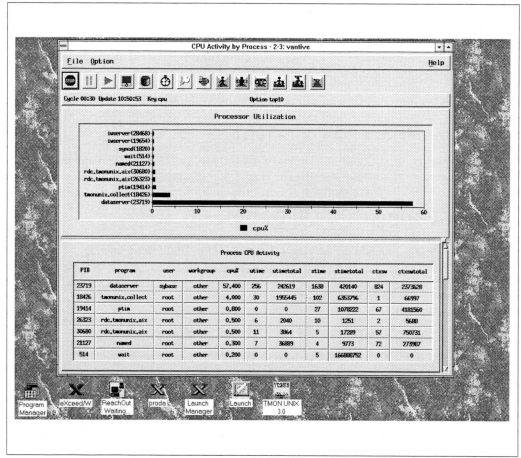

Figure 3-8. CPU Activity by Process

The Monitor for UNIX displays CPU activity by process. It has a graphical part of the report. It also has the capability to show values in a table for those of us who want to know exactly what the numbers. Graphs are pretty, but numbers are real!

Chapter 4: Processor Storage Management

The term *processor storage* is used to refer to the memory inside a computer. Other terms used include *random access memory (RAM), real storage, central storage*, and the oldest term of all, *core memory*. Storage is also used for external disk storage, which is covered in Chapter 5. The terms are often used interchangeably.

Part of the complexity of processor storage management is that most sophisticated operating systems and their subsystems have adopted pooling techniques and preferred storage techniques. These topics are too detailed for this book and are very specific to the operating system. Complete management of processor storage requires you to understand and manage those pools to graduate to a study of how your operating system manages pools after you master these concepts.

For the purposes of this book, I use the term *real storage* to mean the cards or memory chips you place into the computer. Your computing system usually starts with some number of megabytes of real storage and you add more as you need it for performance reasons.

I use the term *virtual storage* to mean the operating system architecture for memory programs access. It usually takes a complete architecture change to vary the virtual storage available. For example, MVS/XA accessed 16 megabytes of virtual storage and MVS/ESA accesses two gigabytes of virtual storage.

For most experienced performance analysts working on mainframes, UNIX platforms, or even PCs, the first rule of thumb for storage management is to buy all the real memory you can afford. First a tip: Normally, I don't like rules of thumb because they tend to oversimplify complex subjects. Figure 4-1, however, gives a rule of thumb that holds some merit: **Memory equals capacity.** One of the reasons I made this into a

MEMORY = CAPACITY

Figure 4-1. Memory Equals Capacity

This figure is just a reminder that the most important thing you can do to almost any platform or operating system is to give it enough memory to operate. If you are running out of capacity on a PC, distributed, or mainframe system, consider adding memory to extend the life of the CPU and I/O subsystems.

figure is to stress this concept. Do you need more capacity? Try adding real storage.

Even if you have more storage than you need on your system today, you eventually will run out. Few of the system administrators I've interviewed ever get all the hardware and software they think is necessary to run a system. If you have unlimited software, hardware, and people budgets, skip this discussion and call or wire me immediately.

If there is any restraint on the CPU and I/O components by the quantity of memory that is available, adding memory is a very good thing to do. You really want a balance of the three resources.

4.1 Virtual Storage

All modern operating systems use *virtual storage* concepts to implement multiprocessing and multiprogramming because CPUs are too fast to be dedicated to a single task and real storage quickly becomes overcommitted with multiple tasks running. Even personal computers use swap techniques to satisfy the needs of multiple tasks running in the CPU.

While virtual storage implementation is very operating-system specific and difficult to cover here, I have included this section to ensure you are aware that there is a virtual storage mapping for your tasks/processes.

4

Virtual storage contains instructions and data. Programmers write their computer programs to perform certain tasks. The instructions (for example, add or subtract) operate on data areas (for example, counters or switches) and information taken from external files from I/O devices, such as direct access storage devices (DASD), printers, tape drives, or terminals.

The computer programs are compiled into machine, object-level, or executable files without using real addresses and are stored in disk files. A program is "loaded" into "virtual storage" (with each virtual storage page frame "backed" by a real storage page frame). Thereafter, a virtual storage frame must be either in a real storage frame or on a "frame" (4-kb record) on disk. This concept is completely explained in "Virtual Storage Concepts," later in this chapter.

4.1.1   Mainframe Virtual Storage

On the mainframe, addresses are specified by using a *register* and a *displacement*. Part of the module loading process is resolution of relocatable addresses to virtual addresses. Virtual addresses don't change.

When the task/process starts up or accesses new virtual storage, real addresses are allocated from a pool of free pages and the dynamic address translation (DAT) hardware is notified that accesses to virtual address xxxxxxxx will be operated on in real storage page yyyyyyyy. Only addresses the program actually needs to use are allocated.

A virtual storage structure sometimes gives the illusion that there is more memory than there actually is real memory in a computer (some large mainframes have two-gigabytes of virtual storage and can have two-gigabytes of real storage!). In this way, ten 500-megabyte task/processes can be loaded into one 32-megabyte real storage as long as the 10 do not need more than 32 megabytes at any one time.

4.1.2 UNIX Virtual Storage

UNIX System V Release 4 implements address spaces divided into *segments*, or *regions*. A segment is a contiguous portion of virtual storage. Types of segments in System V include:

- **Text.** The program being run by the process. Since programs should not modify themselves, this segment is usually marked *read-only* and can be shared by multiple processes for efficiency sake.

- **Data.** The data areas that are modified (marked *read/write*) by the program.

- **Stack.** The process stack where information is maintained when one program calls another.

- **Shared memory.** A data area that is accessible to other processes. This is similar to MVS common storage areas or VM shared segments. This segment is available to the virtual storage areas of other processes.

- **Mapped file.** A file may be mapped into memory segments so the program does not have to do *read* or *write* system calls. The program can read or write to the file by using pointers and the system takes care of the access to an I/O device. This segment is available to the virtual storage areas of other processes.

4.1.3 Storage Overcommitment

I can hear the question, "What if too many tasks/processes are started and their virtual storage demands exceed the real storage's ability to map the virtual storage?"

That's where we start to manage storage. If one or more tasks/processes need to access virtual storage that is not mapped to a real page, then the operating system must act to allocate some to the task/process. Operating systems don't place orders with your friendly computer salesman. Operating systems page and swap real storage page frames, whether they are mainframe or UNIX systems.

4.2 Real Storage

The mainframe System/390 architecture is built on 4,096 characters in a page frame. The value "4,096" is often referred to as 4 kilobytes, or *4 kb*. Early System/360 machines used 2,048 (2 kb) frames, especially for the smaller operating systems, but they are all now 4 kb.

The UNIX architecture is dependent on the architecture of the manufacturer, but generally uses four kilobytes. Get the books for the system you are using or ask your hardware salesman!

The bottom line with real storage is that no multiprogramming operating system/hardware combination has enough real storage to contain all the programs, operating system modules, and data that can run on that system. So, if you want to be a performance tuning guru, start by adding more real storage than your processes or tasks require.

4.2.1 Task/Process Memory States

In Figure 4-2, we see the states in which a task/process may exist during its life.

Sometimes it is in real storage, sometimes it is out of real storage. In this figure, UNIX names are used, but the mainframe environment has the same states and they are translated for you on the outside of the circles. The states shown are:

① **Kernel running.** The operating system kernel is in control and is looking at the queue of ready, in-storage tasks. The mainframe is in supervisor state.

② **User #1 running.** The operating system finds and dispatches User Number 1. This user continues to use the CPU until the program issues a system call or an interrupt takes control of the CPU and

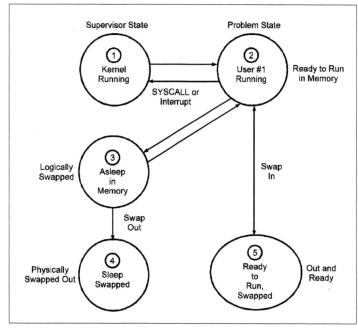

Figure 4-2. Memory States of a Task/Process

A task/process is always loaded into storage at the start of execution.
At ② , the program is running. It gives up control by syscall or
interrupt. At ③ , it may wake up and be dispatched or be swapped
(④) if it waits too long.

dispatches the kernel (or MVS/VM/VSE, in the
case of the mainframe). The task/process is *ready*
to run in memory. On the mainframe, the task is in
problem state.

③**Asleep in memory.** The task/process is
nondispatchable and waiting for something to
happen, but the operating system has not taken its
memory. It may be waiting for a file (I/O
operation) or for another task/process to free up a
resource (enqueue or dequeue on the mainframe).
On the mainframe, the task is logically swapped.

④ **Sleep swapped.** The task/process has been
swapped out to the page or swap file (auxiliary
storage in MVS). No instructions can be executed

4

nor can the process be dispatched until this process is reversed. On the mainframe, this type of task is *physically swapped out*.

⑤ **Ready to run, swapped.** Whatever the task/process was waiting for has now occurred. Note that the operating system had to keep some control blocks in storage to indicate what the task/process was waiting for and where it was located on the external media. For example, the user associated with this task/process may have entered data on the terminal, or the event the task/process was waiting for may have completed. On the mainframe, this task is out and ready. After the swap-in process completes, the task/process is ready to run in memory.

4.3 Memory Management

There really are only three states of a real storage frame. Figure 4-3 shows that the page contains data or instructions of the *system* (UNIX kernel or MVS operating system), the *user* (application code and data

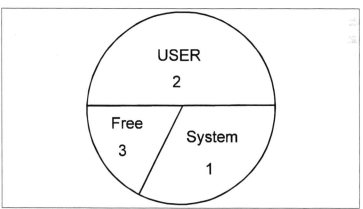

Figure 4-3. Who is Using Memory?

Don't forget that there are only three divisions of storage: system, user, and free (all unused and unassigned storage). A tuning exercise is to determine how much of 1 and 2 storage is unused that can be stolen and moved into the free block.

areas), or *free* (unallocated) storage. I/O buffers can be in either the user area or the system area.

Since it is possible for the parts of a task/process to be in storage and some not, the operating system has *paging* or *swapping* subsystems to handle the pages in real storage and those that need to go in or out of storage. If you have a virtual storage system, you must have a paging subsystem, by definition.

Paging subsystems read and write single pages of real storage to DASD files. This activity is called *demand paging* in the mainframe environment. Paging subsystems are great for interactive tasks/processes that have random access to storage. The drawback to these systems is referred to as *thrashing*, where a task/process requires one page after another, causing the operating system to consume a large portion of the system just to move pages.

Swapping subsystems transfer all the pages for a task/process to and from DASD files. This system is great for batch-like tasks/processes because it gets all of an interrupted task/process out of (or back into) storage at one time. The drawback is that tasks/processes that require a large block of storage can really clog the DASD system when they are swapped out or back into storage.

4.3.1   Mainframe Memory Management

A classic mainframe performance problem occurs when a large job (such as a sort or large test of an online system) is swapped in or out. I have seen 1- to 3-second transaction response time delays due to this problem.

The mainframe environment uses a combination of these two storage management philosophies. MVS/ESA, VM/ESA, and VSE/ESA use both demand paging and swapping to handle the tasks that will be able to use processor storage. For example, in MVS/ESA, if a task is ready to run and in storage, the pages it needs will be brought into storage one at a

4

time as a page fault is detected. If MVS/ESA needs to steal pages from a task, single pages or blocks of pages may be written to the page data sets and freed up for other tasks. If the whole task is to be paged out, block paging routines move multiple pages (12 to many pages) at one time.

All mainframe systems use a concept called *fixed storage*. Important page frames (operating system or user page frames) are locked into storage to prevent them from being stolen by other tasks.

In both the mainframe and UNIX environments, paging/swapping is bad for the health of a system. Too much paging/swapping can be disastrous. To determine how much is too much, ask yourself:

- What is the capacity of my I/O subsystem to do paging? Is the rate of paging exceeding that capacity or causing interference with other work on that path/device?

- Which task/process is causing the activity to the external page/swap data sets?

- Which task/process is being delayed because it needs a page/swap file access to continue? It may even be *thrashing* where the vhand, swapper, statdaemon, or sched daemon processes are using over 1-2% of the processor. These are examples of the virtual memory daemons.

Why are these things important to you? The reason is simple: When the operating system is out of storage, it expends huge amounts of time to move tasks/processes into and out of storage — whether by paging or by swapping. Said another way, when you are short on resources, the shortage is made worse by the management of the shortage. Not a pretty sight.

Table 4-1 shows the types of real storage in the different environments.

Table 4-1. Mainframe vs. UNIX: Storage Management

Environment	Mainframe	UNIX
Operating system	Nucleus and other modules are fixed in storage. Other parts of the operating system are pageable.	Kernel is fixed in storage.
Access methods	Almost all of these are in pageable storage, although they can be fixed by the customer for tuning purposes.	Some parts are in storage, and other parts are pageable.
Programs	Must be in storage for execution, but can be paged or swapped out.	Must be in storage for execution, but can be paged or swapped out.

4.3.2 UNIX Memory Management

The UNIX environment uses either paging or swapping. Systems that send all pages for a process out to DASD are called *swapping systems*. Systems that send only selected pages to a DASD device are called *paging systems*. Some of the programs in the system are pageable and some are not. Some (mostly operating system modules) are fixed in storage from the time the system is started until it terminates.

Some UNIX systems implement a *sticky bit* to indicate fixed pages. If the sticky bit is on, the pages are left in storage after the user is finished with the page.

Real memory in UNIX environments varies from platform to platform. This section concentrates on the metrics available in the various UNIX systems.

Figure 4-4 shows the type of information available in the UNIX environment.

Each platform in the UNIX arena has slightly different data for you to work with. In this case, we are looking at a Sun/OS system. This screen is taken from Landmark's PROBE/X UNIX monitor. Some of this

4

data is available through the UNIX vmstat or sar command.

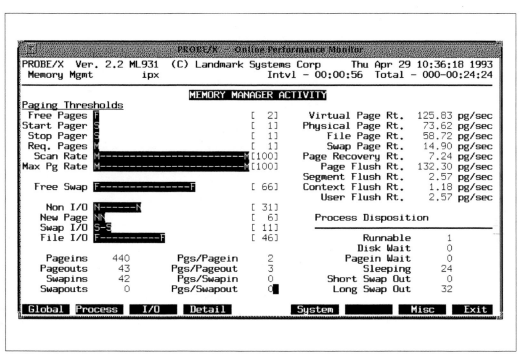

```
┌──────────────────────────────────────────────────────────────────────────┐
│                   PROBE/X   Online Performance Monitor                      │
│PROBE/X  Ver. 2.2 ML931  (C) Landmark Systems Corp      Thu Apr 29 10:36:18 1993│
│ Memory Mgmt            ipx              Intvl - 00:00:56  Total - 000-00:24:24│
│                         MEMORY MANAGER ACTIVITY                             │
│Paging Thresholds                                                           │
│ Free Pages F                          [  2]     Virtual Page Rt.  125.83 pg/sec│
│Start Pager S                          [  1]    Physical Page Rt.   73.62 pg/sec│
│ Stop Pager S                          [  1]        File Page Rt.   58.72 pg/sec│
│ Req. Pages M                          [  1]        Swap Page Rt.   14.90 pg/sec│
│  Scan Rate M----------------------M[100]      Page Recovery Rt.    7.24 pg/sec│
│Max Pg Rate M----------------------M[100]          Page Flush Rt.  132.30 pg/sec│
│                                                Segment Flush Rt.    2.57 pg/sec│
│ Free Swap F--------------F             [ 66]   Context Flush Rt.    1.18 pg/sec│
│                                                   User Flush Rt.    2.57 pg/sec│
│   Non I/O N------N                     [ 31]                                 │
│  New Page NN                          [  6]     Process Disposition         │
│  Swap I/O S-S                         [ 11]     ─────────────────────       │
│  File I/O F---------F                 [ 46]           Runnable        1      │
│                                                      Disk Wait       0      │
│   Pageins    440      Pgs/Pagein    2              Pagein Wait       0      │
│   Pageouts    43      Pgs/Pageout   3                 Sleeping      24      │
│   Swapins     42      Pgs/Swapin    0          Short Swap Out        0      │
│   Swapouts     0      Pgs/Swapout   0           Long Swap Out       32      │
│                                                                            │
│  Global  Process   I/O    Detail          System           Misc    Exit    │
└──────────────────────────────────────────────────────────────────────────┘
```

Figure 4-4. Sample Display of Memory Information

Landmark's PROBE/X UNIX monitor displays paging information from a Sun/OS system.

4.3.2.1   Paging Threshold Fields

This screen shows you the most important things to watch in your system.

- *Free Pages* is the percentage of the free pages of real memory as a function of the total available real memory. This value gives you some idea of how much real storage not in use at this time. Some free storage is not necessary for proper operation. Free storage above that level is *excess capacity*. A note of caution here: **You must understand what is behind this number.** Depending on how the system tracks and manages real storage, this value could give you a false sense of well-being or force you into thinking you need more storage than you really do. We need a few more pieces of information before we continue this discussion. These thresholds usually are set in the kernel parameters and typically cannot be changed dynamically. In mainframe systems, the size of the system is usually applied to specified parameters to modify the thresholds automatically.

- *Start Pager* (from the GPGSLO parameter) is the percentage of real memory that must be available to the system. If the free pages value falls below this value, the pager starts its dirty work: Swapping pages to secondary storage.

- *Stop Pager* (from the GPGSHI parameter) is the percentage of free memory that must be available to the processes for the pager to stop paging out. This is the high threshold value. If the value is too high, the pager will steal too many pages. If it is too low, the pager will stop paging too soon and have to restart again prematurely.

Other metrics maintained by the paging system are Req. Pages, Scan Rate, Max Pg Rate, and Free Swap.

Req. Pages is the percentage of real memory that must be available to ensure that memory requests can be granted.

Scan Rate is the number of passes made by the page-out daemon process relative to the configured maximum rate. This rate is a deciding factor in enabling system swapping.

Max Pg Rate is the number of page-out operations relative to the configured maximum that the page-out daemon process will start in a single scan for pages.

Free Swap is the percentage of pages of free secondary storage available. If swap space runs low, you should configure additional swap areas. This one is serious. The system administrator should check this periodically to ensure that the operating system does not go into emergency mode. In the mainframe, this is the auxiliary storage shortage problem, which causes address spaces to be abnormally terminated or the whole system to crash. UNIX suffers the same fate, sometimes crashing.

4.3.2.2   Paging Request Fields

NON I/O is the percentage of total faults that did not require disk I/O and were satisfied by reclaiming a page from the page cache. In the mainframe environment, this is simply called *page reclaims*. High numbers here may be good news. When a page is marked "free", the data on it is still there. A reclaim occurs when the system marked a page free and then the application went to use the data that was still on the page.

Be sure that your thresholds are not too low. You may specify a number that forces your system to try to get pages before their time. It also may be a precursor to running out of storage. If you see this number grow over time, it may be a warning that you are running out of storage.

New Page is the percentage of total page faults requesting a new page be allocated to the process. In a development environment, this could be a sign of a process that is looping or otherwise using an unreasonable and increasing amount of space.

Swap I/O is the percentage of total page faults that required disk I/O to or from the swap DASD device.

File I/O is the percentage of total faults that required file I/O. These are actually demand page-outs.

4.3.2.3   Paging Activity Fields

Pageins is the number of page-in operations initiated during the current interval.

Pageouts is the number of page-out operations initiated during the current interval.

Pgs/Pagein is the average number of pages paged in during a page-in operation. The system may attempt to prefetch additional pages during each page-in operation.

Pgs/Pageout is the average number of pages paged out during a page-out operation. The system may attempt to optimize page-out by moving multiple adjacent pages during each page-out operation.

Swapins is the number of swap-in operations initiated during the current interval.

Swapouts is the number of swap-out operations initiated during the current interval.

Pgs/Swapin is the average number of pages swapped in during a swap-in operating.

Pgs/Swapout is the average number of pages swapped out during a swap-out operation.

4.3.2.4   Paging Rate Fields

Virtual Page Rt. is the number of page faults per second occurring in the current interval. A page fault occurs when an object mapped into memory is not currently in real memory.

Physical Page Rt. is the number of page faults per second that required physical I/O to resolve. This is another important variable to monitor because it shows the load on your I/O subsystem.

4

File Page Rt. is the number of virtual page faults per second resulting in page-in operations from the file system during the most recent interval.

Swap Page Rt. is the number of virtual page faults per second resulting in page-in or swap-in operations from a swap partition during the most recent interval.

Page Recovery Rt. is the number of pages recovered per second during the most recent interval.

Page Flush Rt. is the number of pages invalidated per second during the current interval.

Segment Flush Rt. is the number of segments invalidated per second during the current interval.

Context Flush Rt. is the number of hardware contexts unloaded per second during the current interval.

User Flush Rt. is the number of user structures invalidated per second during the current interval.

4.3.2.5 Process Disposition Fields

Runnable is the number of in-memory runnable processes. For MVS, this is the number of *in and ready* tasks. This is one of the most important metrics. If you have only a few runnable tasks, the rest of these metrics are probably meaningless. You should use these types of metrics when your system is running near peak load.

Disk Wait is the number of processes waiting for a disk I/O operation to complete. You may think this metric is out of place, but remember that the paging subsystem eventually uses the disk subsystem. If the paging system is hogging the channels and disks, you may see a backlog here.

Pagein Wait is the number of processes waiting for a page-in operation to complete. This is the most important metric in the bunch. Here the processes are being delayed.

Sleeping is the number of processes sleeping. In the mainframe environment, this would be called out and waiting.

Short Swap Out is the number of processes swapped out temporarily. This number is also a problem. It indicates that the operating system was short on storage and has thrown out these lower priority process/tasks.

Long Swap Out is the number of processes swapped out during long sleeps. These processes will not even be swapped in until they awaken. In the mainframe, these are terminal wait or some long-term wait such as waiting for an enqueue to be freed up.

4.4 Virtual Storage Concepts

Each implementation of virtual storage is different. This section discusses different concepts implemented in UNIX and MVS (or mainframe) systems.

Almost all operating system support programs are shared by multiple tasks/processes. One copy of a program image in memory is required no matter how many tasks/processes are executing it. On the mainframe, this is called *reentrant* programming. In UNIX, all C programs are reentrant.

Reentrant programming provides two benefits. The first is storage savings; the second is speed and efficiency. If 100 tasks/processes are each using their own copy of a 10 kb program, one megabyte of real storage is required to hold all of the copies. If you had less than one megabyte, those programs might steal pages from each other. It would not be impossible for Page 1 of the shared program to be stolen from Process 1 and replaced by the same Page 1 from Process 2.

This situation is true for almost all subsystems. In
IBM CICS systems, one of the most important things
you can do is to ensure that often-used programs
remain in storage. In mainframe operating systems,
you do well to keep (or *page fix*) commonly used
programs in real storage. The same applies to most
UNIX systems.

4.4.1   Virtual vs. Real Addresses

Figure 4-5 shows the relationship between virtual
storage and real storage.

In the box on the left, a 12-megabyte virtual address
space operating system is pictured. In this case, the
kernel is assigned six megabytes and the process or
user address space, another six megabytes. Note that

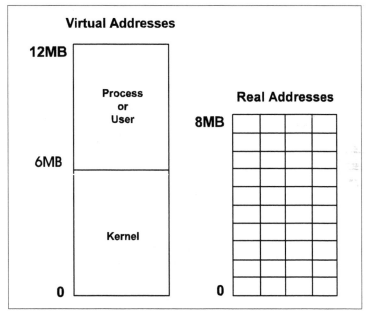

Figure 4-5. Virtual and Real Addresses

*All virtual operating systems are based on two components. First, on
the right, is a block of real addresses. In this case, eight megabytes of
real storage is available. The operating system has one or more virtual
address spaces for programs. In this case, one 12-megabyte address
space is shown with the kernel from zero to six megabytes and the
task/process occupying the top six megabytes.*

this arrangement is different from the mainframe environment, in which the operating system usually is spread throughout virtual storage. MVS, for example, has areas low in the storage area spanning the 16-megabyte line (private storage area (PSA) is the first 4,096 bytes), and areas spread throughout the private and extended areas up to two gigabytes.

The physical machine has eight megabytes of real storage. This is the amount of storage that you or your company bought when you purchased or upgraded the processor complex. You might ask, "Is eight megabytes enough to support a 12-megabyte virtual address?" The answer is, "It depends." What if there were 50 12-megabyte virtual users? The answer would be "No."

4.4.2   Page-Outs and Page-Ins

Before we can answer the question, "Is this enough real storage?", we must see what is going on inside the system. Let's look in-depth at what happens to pages.

Figure 4-6 shows the first thing that might happen to a page frame: a *page-out* and then a *page-in*.

① A page frame is in real storage and has not been used during the last cycle (either no instruction or data was read from the page or no data was written to the page). The referenced bit is turned off by the hardware.

② The operating system, in searching through all real pages, finds the referenced bit turned off and updates a table to say that the page has not been referenced during this cycle. This unreferenced value grows until the kernel needs some page frames.

③ The page is paged out of storage onto a DASD device to wait for the process to try to access the page again. In some cases, the page may never be used again in the life of a process. One example of

4

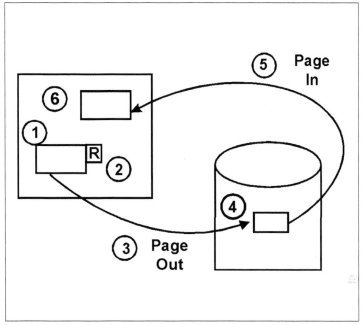

Figure 4-6. What Can Happen to a Page

A page frame in use by a task/process can be in storage, paged out to DASD for holding, or paged back in. Note that the page was in frame ① and came back into page frame ⑥. The real page frame is not important to the program as the hardware and operating system team take care of the relocation calculations.

this is initialization instructions that are executed once and never touched again.

④ The page resides on the page or swap data set.

⑤ Another attempt is made to reference the page. The kernel performs a file I/O to bring the page back into storage.

⑥ The page is now in storage and available to the process.

4.4.3   Page Aging

Let's take a closer look at the *page aging* process shown in Figure 4-7.

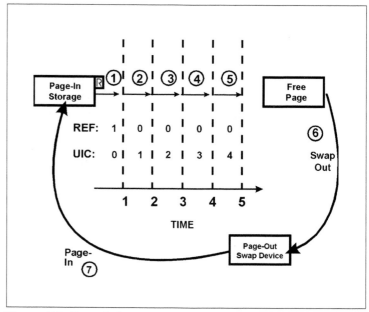

Figure 4-7. Page Aging

If you understand page aging, you will understand how to manage storage. As time marches from ① to ⑤ above, the page in storage is unused for four periods for an unreferenced interval count of 4. If the operating system is stealing page frames four seconds or older, the page is marked either free (if the page was a read-only page that has a valid copy on some disk file) or available for page-out (if the page was changed).

① The page is in storage and has just been referenced. The unreferenced interval count (UIC) is set to 0. (The UNIX equivalent to the UIC is the `lotsfree` page steal variable and the *GPGSLO* tunable parameter.) The referenced bit is on.

② The kernel takes a timer interrupt and goes around real storage to turn off the referenced bits. The UIC counter for this page is set to 1.

③ The kernel repeats the above and adds 1 to the counter of the number of cycles since this page was referenced. The unreferenced count is now 2.

4

④ The previous routine is repeated and the unreferenced count is now 3.

⑤ The kernel is looking in all the right places for pages and decides that every page with a count of 4 or more is a candidate for stealing. This page is marked for stealing and will be swapped out or paged out depending on the implementation.

Until the page is actually moved out and *used by another process*, the page could be *reclaimed* by the original process.

⑥ A page-out is performed and the page frame is now free.

⑦ The owning task tries to access the page and is placed in a wait state while the page is brought back into the processor. Only now can the process be redispatched. Remember from previous discussion that the page will probably not go back into the same real page frame.

4.4.4 Locality of Reference

Figure 4-8 shows an important part of how often a process will be paging.

Assume that the process exists on eight pages of storage. When the process is first dispatched, some portion of the program is brought into storage. In most cases, the entire program is brought in. The probability of a page fault between Steps 1, 2, and 3 is very small. In other words, if Page *A1* is brought into storage with Page *A2*, there will be no page fault as the program progresses.

What about the work areas at *A3* and *A4*? If they are not used, they may be paged out. They may result in a page fault if they are not referenced quickly by the program. At 4, the program asks the user for input. Several seconds later, the program tries to compare WORK1 with WORK2. One or both may be paged out and the process, just revived, waits for the paging

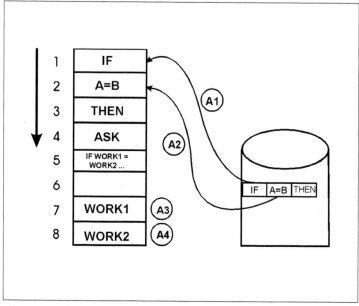

Figure 4-8. Locality of Reference

Some applications should consider locality of reference in their design. The ones to be concerned with are frequently used applications that are called by many other applications. This example shows a program that is eight pages long. (This is an exaggeration: The "IF" statement does not take 4,096 bytes!) All eight segments of the program are brought into storage at program invocation (A1 and A2 show the start of the process). The program then waits for a long time at ④. Segments ⑦ and ⑧ may get paged out of storage (A3 and A4) while waiting. After the operator replies, the task/process will be dispatched and page fault at step ⑤ — another reason for reasonably sized programs.

supervisor. This is called *locality of reference*. Programs should be kept small so program and data areas are in the same page(s). (Reenterable programming can't allow this situation to occur and is a more complex topic than can be addressed here.)

4.4.5   Demand Paging

All mainframe systems work with *demand paging* for many of their paging requests. Figure 4-9 shows demand paging types of UNIX paging systems.

① A user page is stolen and ② written to DASD storage for saving. ③ The page exists on a block of

storage in the paging file area. ④ A page from this or
another process is stolen and ⑤ written to DASD
storage for saving. ⑥ The page exists on a block of
storage in the paging file area. ⑦ If Page 3 is needed,
it must be paged in.

Note that two complete operations had to be
performed to move two pages from real storage into
auxiliary storage. It is bad enough that the kernel
software had to do two complete loops of software,
but the time it takes the I/O subsystem to process the
two I/O requests is far longer in duration.

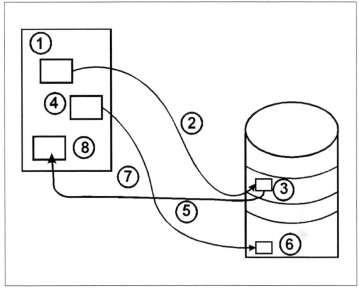

Figure 4-9. Demand Paging: Page-Out and Page-In

*The first of two types of paging is shown here. A page exists at ①. It is
stolen and paged out at ②. A second page, at ④, is stolen and written
to DASD at ⑤. Two pages require two I/O operations.*

4.4.6   Block Paging

A better way to move multiple pages is called *block
paging*. Figure 4-10 shows all three pages being stolen
and going to the paging file in one operation.

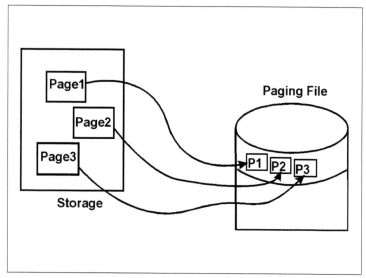

Figure 4-10. Block Paging

This is an example of the second type of paging. Three pages are to be stolen. They are moved to DASD with a single I/O operation. This is a very efficient method of paging. Its drawback is that the device is busy for the full time of the I/O operation.

The way that the operating system does this is to disable all interruptions and search through storage looking for pages to steal. Remember that it does not matter which real storage page is used for which task/process. In other words, one page could be used for Process 1 and the page right next to it could be used for another process.

The same can be said for page slots on the physical media used to save pages. Slot 1 could hold a page from Process 1 and Slot 2 could hold a page from another task/process.

Why is this important? Efficiency. If the operating system can move three blocks in one I/O operation, the second and third blocks are read or written without significant overhead and in the shortest possible time. (This is the closest we come to a free lunch!)

DASD tuning is not part of this discussion, but you may know that DASD spins at a fixed rate (either 3,600 , 4,200, or 7,200 revolutions per minute). Each revolution takes an enormous amount of time (for example, 16 milliseconds) compared to CPU instructions (microseconds or nanoseconds). If the operating system moves all three blocks at one time, they probably can be accomplished in one revolution. If they are moved separately, they probably require at least three revolutions — a triple eternity.

4.4.7 Addressing

Figure 4-11 shows how operating systems perform virtual addressing.

Each process has a set of control blocks that map out the virtual storage available to the task/process. If the

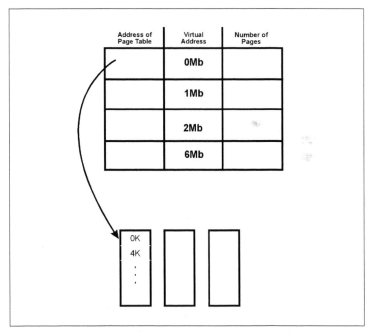

Figure 4-11. Operating System Virtual Addressability

Both the hardware and software need access to a table that either points a virtual address to a real page frame (the hardware will translate and act on the instruction) or to a page or swap location (the operating system must page in the frame).

architecture describes a 16-megabyte address space, the addressing must provide for 24 bits of address. This was MVS/370 and the 24-bit mode of MVS/XA and MVS/ESA. If the architecture defines two gigabytes of storage, the addressing must provide for 31 bits of address. The mainframe 31-bit mode of MVS/ESA is an example of this.

In the figure, the top table contains the addresses and pointers needed to access either real storage page frames (on the bottom of the figure) or some location on the page and swap subsystem. If the virtual address is pointing to a real storage page frame, the hardware can execute the instructions or work on the data in the page. If the virtual storage is not pointing to a real storage page frame, the activity is interrupted and a *page fault* occurs. The operating system must be used to allocate a page if it has never been used or to read the page into storage if it has been *stolen*, or paged out, of storage.

4.4.8   System/390 Virtual Storage

Figure 4-12 shows the System/390 dynamic address processing. Dynamic address translation (DAT) for all System/390 operating systems is shown. MVS divides the two gigabytes of virtual storage into 2,048 1-megabyte segments (11 bits). Each megabyte segment has 256 page frames (8 bits) and each page is 4,096 (12 bits).

Storage is often an overlooked area of performance tuning. It sneaks up on you and can cause you great grief if you are not diligent in watching it. Good luck on your quest to keep your systems running well!

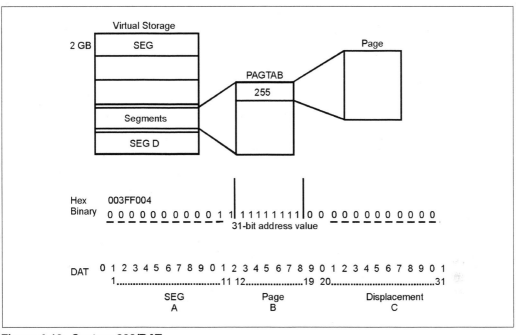

Figure 4-12. System 390/DAT

Another picture of virtual storage mapping. A 2-gigabyte address space is mapped using 11 bits for the 2,048 segments, 8 bits for the 256 pages, and 12 bits for the 4,096 bytes in a page.

The Monitor for UNIX provides a number of reports that show storage metrics. Figure 4-13 shows page faults, page-ins, and page-outs over time. One of the things you will want to do is monitor storage during your peak times to your numbers during busy time. This graph shows page faults peaking at 225 with an average of about 100. Is that good? You can't tell. If your users are happy during this period, then the system is running fine. Note that this graph was created using an artificial load. Your system may gag if it runs this high.

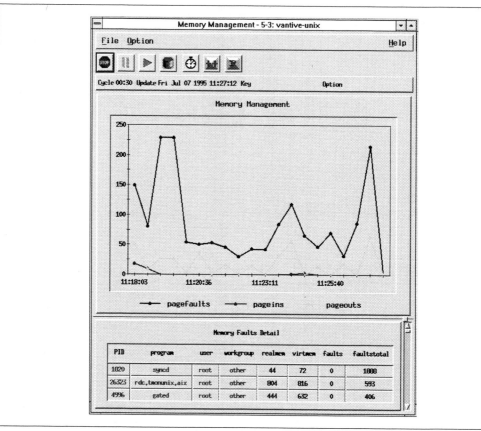

Figure 4-13. Memory Used by Program, User, or Work Group

*Who is using memory? **The Monitor** for UNIX displays memory allocation at points of time so you can see who is using memory. Then you decide if they are good or bad!*

Chapter 5: Input/Output Management

After CPU utilization and real storage are tuned and allocated according to your company's desires, the I/O resource needs to be managed. I/O management provides two significant challenges. First, over 80% of all performance problems are caused by elongated I/O response time. Second, I/O performance tuning requires constant monitoring and reaction. This chapter provides insight into how similar I/O management is in MVS and UNIX — from file structure to devices.

5.1 File Structure

MVS and UNIX file structures are very similar. From a user perspective, there is one view of data. In MVS, this begins with the *master catalog*, which all data accesses must pass through. *User catalogs* are used to subdivide data structures. Data set names can be up to 44 characters long, with eight character groups separated by periods. A data set name is unique in the master catalog hierarchy.

The UNIX file structure — the *file system* — begins with the *root* as represented by the regular slash (as opposed to the backwards slash used in the PC environment). Figure 5-1 shows the UNIX structure. [MVS readers, think of the root as the master catalog, as all user-available disk space is accessed via the root. VM readers, think of the root as the user directory.] *Subdirectories* are used to subdivide data structures. Names are separated by a *slash* (for example, /user02/junk/cmd). UNIX data set names can be in *8+3 format* (1- to 8-character name, period, 1- to 3-character suffix; similar to personal computers) or much longer (32 characters).

If the pathname starts with a slash, then the path starts in the root directory. You move up in the tree with a double period (..). All other paths start in the current directory and move down the tree.

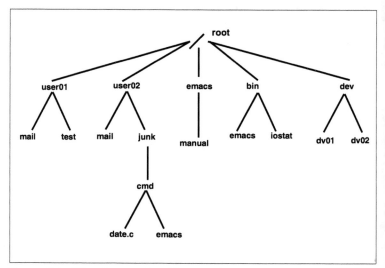

Figure 5-1. Files from a User Perspective

*UNIX, like MVS, begins with a single pointer called the root. In MVS, it
is the master catalog. In this example, there are two user subdirectories.
Note that user02 has a copy of the emacs text editor and the common
(/bin) directory has a second copy. Note also that devices (on the far right)
are just a special type of file.*

Like MVS, UNIX can contain more than one copy of a
program if the copies exist in different directories. In
MVS, STEPLIB and JOBLIB statements are used to
route the program search. In UNIX, the order of
directories in the search path determines which one is
found first.

In MVS, there is only one name for a file because the
name of the file is in the volume table of contents
(VTOC) or the disk points to the beginning of the file
(or an extension of the file on second and subsequent
disks). **In UNIX, a file may have several names!** The
name is nothing more than a pointer to a file
description. Think of UNIX names like aliases in
mainframe partitioned data sets (PDS). One member
can have several names.

File ownership in UNIX is similar to mainframe RACF
(or RACF-like) security. Files have both a user owner
and a group owner. It is best if you establish groups

and use them for access privileges. That way a change to the group definition changes the access for all members of that group — even in the Novell network environment. (It's amazing how a good idea — a *mainframe* idea — spreads!)

In UNIX, everything is a file. A "file" is a continuous string of bytes terminated by an end-of-file. Some UNIX file categories are:

- *Plain files,* such as ASCII text, binary data files, and program files, which most applications use.

- *Pipe,* an interprocess communication facility. Data is received as input from a process and passed to another process on a first-in-first-out basis.

- *Directory files,* which are binary files that contain pointers to other files and directories. [MVS readers, think of these as user catalogs.]

- *Special files,* which are really I/O devices and are covered "5.2 Devices," later in this chapter.

- *Links,* which enable a single file to be referred to by multiple names. These are similar to alias names for members of a mainframe partitioned data set.

- *Sockets,* which are special files used for communication between processes. For example, the /dev/printer socket is often used to send lines of print to the pd program (the line-printer spooling daemon process).

- *Named pipes,* another interprocess communication method that allows applications to open pipes by name.

5.1.1 Access Methods

The mainframe has a rich and well-documented set of file structures, which are referred to as *access methods*. All of the mainframe access methods can be contained on a single spindle or disk. The topic is too broad to be covered here (see *MVS Concepts and Facilities,* mentioned in the preface, for a discussion), but I have listed the various access methods here for your information.

- **Sequential Access Method (SAM)**. SAM files have records placed in a physical rather than logical order. Sequential files are created one record after another. Magnetic tape files are the best example. UNIX programmers can equate this to a piping of the records from one program to another.

- **Indexed Sequential Access Method (ISAM)**. ISAM is a very old access method for files written in sequence according to a key that is part of the record. The record may be retrieved directly by looking up the key in an index.

- **Basic Direct Access Method (BDAM)**. BDAM is also a very old access method for direct access of records. Since the access methodology is left up to the programmer, it has long since fallen out of favor because it is very complex to implement and maintain.

- **Partitioned Access Method (PAM)**. PAM records contain a directory (maintained in alphabetic order) and a part of the file to hold members. Each *member* is a small sequential file, which is most likely a source or parameter data file and allows cost-effective access to many files on a disk. PDS/E (extended) is an efficient implementation of a PAM file.

- **Virtual Storage Access Method (VSAM)**. VSAM is the most widely used type of file. It can be accessed sequentially (relative record data set (RRDS)) or directly (keyed sequential data set (KSDS)). VSAM on the mainframe is similar to UNIX database files like those of Sybase, Oracle, and Informix.

5.1.2   UNIX File Systems

UNIX uses the term *file systems* to describe the data stored on its discs. This is the most intriguing part of UNIX. The IBM mainframe defined access methods and very few vendors tried to create new or better ones. UNIX, on the other hand, declares that file system access is a callable function and, therefore, each month brings out new file systems. A file called /etc/vfstab lists all of the file systems that should be automatically mounted when the system is booted. The kernel maintains a list of the file systems it knows are mounted in a file called /etc/mnttab, which is updated by the *mount* and *unmount* commands.

You won't see detailed descriptions of these file systems because some are proprietary, some are mysterious, and some are elusive. Here is another area where the user community should gather information to compare and contrast these file systems. In some cases, you get the file system when you use a proprietary package. Unless you understand how the file system acts, how are you going to manage? Want to strike fear into the heart of your friendly salesman? Add a clause in the RFP to explain any file systems and the management techniques used for their response to your proposal!

- **UNIX File System (UFS).** When you read a general discussion of UNIX, this is the file system you will see documented. It has a structure similar to the IBM DASD format in that it has *inodes* (VTOC entries) that point to the data sets.

- **Virtual File System (vfs).** This is the generic name used for all types of file systems.

- **Sun's Network File System (NFS).** NFS is probably the most important of the file systems (it is in use by most UNIX systems). The spindle of the file system resides on another physical box under the control of an entirely different UNIX. The benefit is that you can centralize data to one location. The failing is that your I/O operations depend entirely on the other system *and* the network. **Every physical I/O must go over the network.**

- **AT&T's Network File System (RFS).** [Remember the part in the preface about this being a work in progress? Well, I need some information on this type of file system.]

- **Project Andrew's File System (AFS).** AFS was the first of the designed file systems to overcome access problems with NFS files. AFS keeps buffers (and disc backing) for NFS files on the local machine. This way the user is only accessing a remote server if the buffer does not have the requested buffer. But this brings up synchronization problems. What if the remote system updated the buffer that is in this local machine? What about writes?

- **Distributed File System (DFS).** The Open System Foundation (OSF) folks have built another system similar to AFS in that it has local buffers defined for network devices.

Why all of this interest in making NFS work better? First of all, NFS gives great flexibility to placing information where it is best maintained. Performance implications loom. First is the problem of access. If you have many people moving buffers from a remote location, the network may choke. If you have many users just asking to look at the file system, the NFS daemons may spawn many times over to handle the load and cause problems. More on this in Chapter 7.

- **High-Sierra File System (HFS or hsfs).** hsfs is the format used for CD/ROM devices. It has many different versions. One of the more important is the Young Minds' *rockridge* format, a proprietary, but sharable extension to the ISO 9660 standard that allows the long names used in UNIX, not just the 8.3 format described in ISO 9660.

- **Journal File System (JFS)**. JFS is most widely used by database systems.

- **Loopback File System (lofs)** [Again I need to find out what this is and why it is used.]

- **PC/DOS File System (pcfs)** The pcfs is used when a UNIX system is going to access a PC-based spindle.

5.2 Devices

5

The MVS environment supports many types of devices. Almost all of them are *count-key-data (CKD) devices* on block multiplexer channels. VM and VSE (and, to some extent, MVS) allow *fixed-block-architecture (FBA) devices*, which predetermine the physical block size on the disk surface (for example, 512 bytes).

Devices in UNIX are similar to mainframe devices. UNIX systems use two types of devices. *Block special files* (for example, disks and tapes) read and write physical blocks of storage. *Character special files* — usually unbuffered I/O — are terminals either local or out in a network.

The I/O environment in a UNIX-based processor is dependent on the manufacturer's hardware architecture. In most cases, it is fixed-block architecture. In some cases, it is exactly like the MVS environment (as in AIX running on a System/390 processor complex) and, in some cases, vastly different (as in SCO UNIX running on a personal computer).

The discussion of the relative merits of fixed-block devices versus count-key-data devices is an important one, but too lengthy for this book. See *DASD: IBM's Direct Access Storage Devices*, mentioned in the preface, for a discussion.

5.2.1   Hardware Configuration

Both operating systems (indeed all operating systems, save one — NST[1]) require the system administrator to provide configuration data. In both, you specify devices by:

- **Hard-coded configuration**. In MVS, it is in the I/O generation as developed at SYSGEN time. In UNIX, it is placed into files and compiled and linked into the kernel code.

- **Dynamic reconfiguration**. In the latest versions of MVS, devices can be added dynamically. In UNIX, administrators can supply configuration information after the system is running and the kernel changes the internal tables.

- **Self-defining devices.** In UNIX, certain devices allow the kernel to recognize when the devices are installed, then the kernel reads the hardware switches and adds the devices to the configuration. In MVS, dynamic allocation of devices is similar to those self-defining devices.

5.2.2   Hardware Interrupts: Talking to the Devices

Figure 5-2 shows the hardware/software relationships between MVS and UNIX. In the mainframe environment, one I/O supervisor (IOS, or *first-level interrupt handler (FLIH)*) handles an interrupt and passes the request to a *second-level interrupt handler (SLIH)*. In UNIX, the kernel modules that control devices are known as *device drivers*. Usually, each type of device has one device driver. DASD devices are handled by a DASD device driver, tapes by a tape driver, and so forth.

In MVS, once devices are known to the system, they can be used by any task in the system. In most cases

---

[1]   Only IBM systems engineers will probably recognize "NST." It was an IBM diagnostic program, IPL'ed from tape. It recognized all devices, told you what devices they were, and asked your advice.

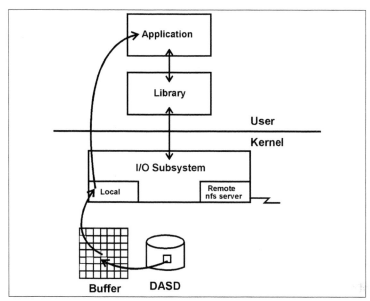

Figure 5-2. Buffering I/O Requests

UNIX has the kernel reading and writing files, just like MVS does but sometimes the physical records come into a common buffer (as pictured here) and sometimes the physical records come into private storage for a particular application. Database applications are more likely to manage their own buffers.

(for example, DASD devices), they are shared by all tasks. In some cases (for example, tape drives and some byte-oriented teleprocessing devices), they are dedicated to a particular task. In UNIX, the kernel, acting for a process, opens a device, closes a device, reads a device, and writes to a device.

The handling of a device shows a subtle, but important, difference between MVS and UNIX. In MVS, the application may need intimate knowledge of the workings and rules of operation. All units of work in UNIX are procedures that are defined at a very high level. They do not know or care about devices.

On the other hand, the reason UNIX shields the application is that UNIX supports only one block size and one (native) access method. MVS applications wouldn't care about device geometry, either, if all devices were 512-byte blocks, accessed sequentially. In a sense, UNIX applications are device-aware, but to a very small range of devices.

Which brings up a thought about the future of UNIX. Early IBM Virtual Machine (VM) operating systems had fixed-block (800-byte) architecture. As VM grew from a single-use (interactive computing) to a multipurpose, full-function operating system, the end user needed, and was given, the opportunity to select other physical block sizes (1,024; 4,096; and 8,192) and access methods (VSAM). Will UNIX be asked to provide similar flexibility?

5.2.3   Hardware Reads and Writes

In MVS, a physical data block is read into or written from a real storage page frame allocated to the application. Access method routines may pull out and move records into the program's buffer, but generally once read, they are available only to the task.

One drawback to basic MVS file structure is that if two tasks want to read the same block of data on a file, there are two copies of the block in storage. This is not true of partition data set/extended (PDS/E), of data in virtual (DIV), or for DB2 data sets.

Some implementations of UNIX are based on the concept of one buffer shared by multiple processes. Thus, if process 59 reads a block and process 90 wants to read the same block, UNIX will use the same buffer to move the data to the user area for process 59 and then move another copy to the buffer area for process 90 (see Figure 5-2).

The difference lies in the architecture. MVS wants all I/O to be performed into or out of task private storage. UNIX wants all I/O to be controlled by the kernel into a central pool of buffers. You can think of MVS as a server, UNIX as a controller.

UNIX also supports the concept of remote I/O operations (see Figure 5-3). The application on System A opens a file identified to UNIX as a remote file located on System B. The kernel goes out over the network via an *nfs daemon process* to a remote kernel and gets or writes a block of data.

Large data files may be a problem for this type of access. As large volumes are transferred across the network, it may become bogged down with data transfer and experience interference with terminal access.

5

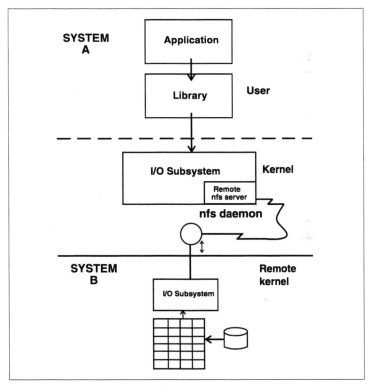

Figure 5-3. UNIX Remote I/O Access

UNIX also supports the concept of remote access for files. In this example, System A has a path defined as being on System B. When an application reads or writes blocks in the file, the kernel uses the network file server (nfs) daemon to send the request to System B.

5.2.4   Physical Block Sizes

In MVS, the end user specifies the physical block size of the files he creates. This has some good and some not-so-good attributes. The end user can overload direct access devices by specifying very small block sizes, such as 80-byte blocks. Or, he can make his processes very efficient by specifying a very large block size, such as a half-track file (for DASD) or 32-kilobyte files (for tape).

In UNIX, the system administrator specifies the block size for a file system. This is not the same as the physical block size set by the hardware manufacturer. For example, an administrator may specify a 2,048-byte block size for an FBA device with 512-byte blocks, which would fit nicely with four physical blocks being allocated to a single logical block.

As with all architectural decisions, solving one problem may lead to creation of another. There are always trade-offs. Once the logical size is set, it is fixed until you reformat the disk and file system.

If a small block size is specified, disk space is wasted and many more physical reads may be necessary for the complete file. If large sizes are specified, empty blocks may waste real storage as the records are read into storage.

Some UNIX implementations have tried to overcome this dichotomy by specifying *fragged methodology*. In this environment, a large block (for example, 4,096 bytes) can be shared by several files, but requires a significant amount of overhead and, in at least one case that I know of, it only makes matters worse.

Figure 5-4 shows a more complete view of UNIX I/O buffering. UNIX, like mainframe software, has user, kernel, and hardware areas of interaction.

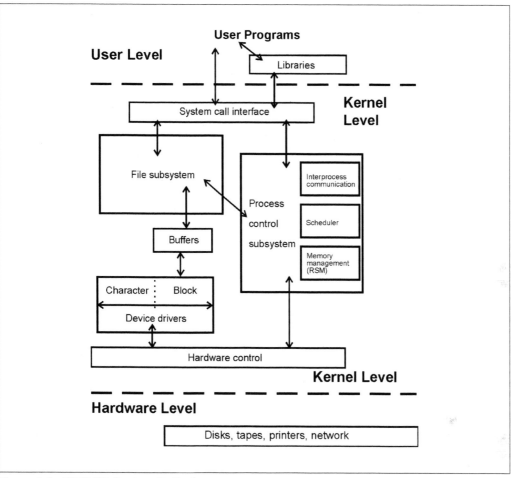

Figure 5-4. UNIX I/O System Buffering

A more complex view of buffering is shown here. Just like MVS, there are three levels. A user level at the top, where application programs open, read, and write files. In the middle, the kernel level contains schedulers, memory management (real storage management), and file subsystems (IOS). The hardware (disks, tapes, printers, and the network) is at the bottom. Just like MVS, device drivers handle I/Os from different types of devices.

5.3 Summary

Table 5-1 summarizes mainframe and UNIX I/O concepts.

Table 5-1: Mainframe vs. UNIX: Input/Output		
Concept	**Mainframe**	**UNIX**
Interrupt handler	Input/Output Supervisor.	Device drivers.
System configuration	System generation or I/O generation.	System configuration parameters such as process table size, inode table size, file table size, number of buffers for buffer pool, and device addresses.
Where will device place physical blocks?	In buffer allocated for exclusive use of task.	In buffer allocated from kernel buffer pool.
Buffering	Each task has buffers for files.	Kernel has buffer for all devices. Every process read/write means a CPU copy operation. Some I/O can go directly to the process's area to bypass the copy.
Remote files	Either loosely or tightly coupled to share files on DASD, or the whole task must be shipped to the remote processor complex.	Satellite processes (remote computers without peripherals), Newcastle (special file names point to remote UNIX kernels), or fully distributed (kernel recognizes remote files).
Physical blocks	CKD or fixed-block architecture.	Fixed-block architecture specified by the administrator.
Common input file	*//SYSIN DD *.*	Standard input file.
Common output file	*//SYSOUT DD SYSOUT=A.*	Standard output file.
Common message file	*//SYSOUT DD SYSOUT=A.*	Standard error file.

Eventually, you will have to do in-depth studies of your I/O subsystem. Figure 5-5 shows one of **The Monitor** for UNIX reports on a UNIX system. You can display information about each of the file systems and the entire disc itself.

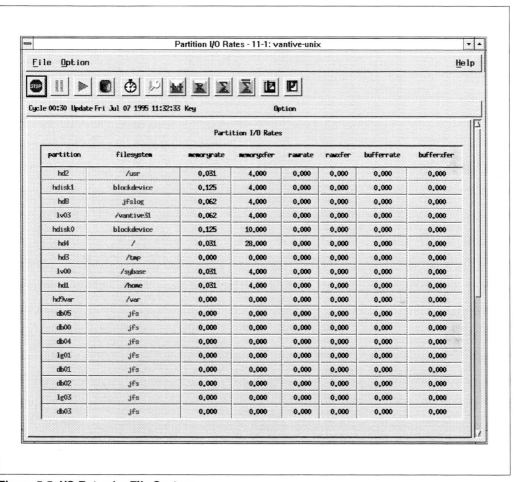

Figure 5-5. I/O Rates by File System

The Monitor for UNIX shows information about the file system and the drives. Note the "memrate and "memxfer" versus "rawrate" and "rawxfer". You normally do not see both of these. The "mem" ones show normal I/O and the "raw" shows low level I/O such as database I/O.

PART III: Systems Management

This part of the book concentrates on the systems management portions of our two platforms. Since I come from a background of performance and systems management in a mainframe environment, presentation of the material is biased in that direction.

You can look at systems management as being similar to Abraham Maslow's hierarchy of needs from *Theory of Motivation:*   Physiological needs such as food (will this system work at all?), safety needs (security), social needs (networking), esteem needs (performance and troubleshooting), and self-actualization (capacity planning). For this discussion, I will assume you have picked your platform correctly and the system you are implementing or looking at actually works.

Security comes first as Chapter 6. Many of my contemporaries agree with me that security is not just for auditors with green eye shades.[1] Security is for you, every one of you.

Performance is a very broad term. As treated in Chapter 7, it could even be viewed as facilities management because I concentrate on the hardware aspects of performance management. I find too often that hardware just *grows* and causes problems because some people only care if it is hooked up.

Networking should come next, but that part of the book is still in the building phase. If you are reading this and are a networking guru, have you ever wanted to be an author? Call me.

Capacity planning is another part still in the building phase.

---

[1]   For you youngsters in the crowd, auditors and accountants in your father's day worked on handwritten ledgers. They used green eye shades to keep the glare out of their eyes.

Chapter 6: Security

Whole books have been written on security and I
don't intend to duplicate that research here. A simple
definition by Mark Nelson of IBM's RACF design and
special projects team (SHARE, February 28, 1995,
Session 4955) is good enough for our purposes here:

> *The protection of data from accidental or malicious
> disclosure, modification, or destruction.*

That's a tall order, but for a starter, let's look at
security from 47,000 feet.

6.1 Security Standards

Security is in the eyes of the beholder. In the data
processing industry, security means what the U.S.
Department of Defense (DOD) and associated
agencies say it means. In 1985, DOD published the
Orange Book, which specified a hierarchy of security
controls spanning three levels.

C level. This level is the minimum a system can be
labeled when the owners of the system prove it can
protect against several attacks. C1 is the basic level
and C2 is the commercial standard here in 1996. The
National Computer Security Center (NCSC) does not
certify C-level security any more but relies on the
manufacturer to state (and stand by) its claims.

6

Which brings home the notion that you must
understand these security levels and exactly what
they mean. Windows NT Server has C2-level security
unless it is connected to a network! You must ask
questions and be sure you know the answers if
security is important to you and your company.

B level. This level adds advanced privacy protection
facilities. It is the level that most mission-critical
systems should strive for. It is easy to make MVS a B1
system. It is relatively hard to make UNIX a B-level
system. I wonder who does this? Anyone you know?

A level. An A-level system meets the majority of the most sensitive national security requirements. The system's engineers must have it certified by the NCSC.

6.2   Security Functions

In this book, I have focused on the following functional areas of security.

- **User authorization.** The system should make access decisions based on a person's identity. That identity is developed from a *login* command supplying a *user ID* and a *password*. User authorization is the first area in which most security systems fail: Either they don't require passwords or the user ID and password are shared by multiple individuals.

- **User separation and combination.** You should be able to specify a user's privileges and to group users together to make maintenance easy.

- **Resource access control.** You should be able to limit access to data or services to a particular user or group of users.

- **Event or transaction logging.** A consistent (and permanent) record of important transactions must be provided. Thus, failed logon attempts should be logged and maybe acted upon.

- **Process separation.** One user's applications must be separated from interfering with another user's data either by accident or deliberately. Your data should not be compromised by another user unless you give that user explicit or implicit authority.

- **Controlled entry and exit.** Entry to and exit from any transaction accessing data must be controlled and accounted for.

- **Controlled transactions.** Programs that operate on data or services must be controlled. Said another way, you should know who is executing programs that access data or services.

6.3 Why Security?

Security is not an auditor function nor a technical function; it is a corporate function. Someone must decide, for the corporation as a whole, what must be protected and how much the corporation is going to spend on that protection. Every level of security costs something. The more secure you make something, the more that security will cost you.

Nothing can be totally secure. It was reported that many years ago, an executive of Johnson and Johnson (who makes BandAids and other first aid supplies) challenged an executive of IBM to "make MVS totally secure." The IBM executive replied, "I will give you the same guarantee you make of your sterile products: MVS is totally secure until you open the box and install the operating system." (Each BandAid was marked "Guaranteed sterile until opened.")

I maintain that security is a must-have feature of any mission-critical computing system. Security must be an integral part of any full-function operating system. Why, you ask?

Security is not always about keeping people out. It is also a means of providing access to information that people need. The single greatest threat to security of your data is human carelessness by the people you see every day, starting with the person looking in the mirror. Input errors create bad data. Data sets scratched by mistake cause problems. Data sometimes gets updated when you don't want it updated. Sometimes the software does not even tell you it updated the data! As the cartoon character Pogo said many years ago while standing in his boat, "We have seen the enemy and they is us!" Who of you reading this has not scratched a data set or lost some set of files? When we get to superusers and

6

RACF special users later in this chapter, I share a tip I have always used to keep me out of trouble.

6.4   Security History

Some say that MVS and other mainframe operating systems that use RACF interfaces are the most secure operating systems ever devised.

Some writers say that UNIX is not a secure system and cannot be made secure. Indeed, in the first half of the 1990s, most UNIX systems administrators found there was no enterprisewide UNIX security. Public domain software programs provide a basis to build a departmental security system but, when multiple departments are linked together, the result is an unsecure system. A homegrown, locally implemented security system does not cut the mustard either.

Neither of these statements is true. In fact, the opposite may be true. And your experience is probably somewhere in between.

Before we can separate the myths from the truth, let's begin with some background on MVS and UNIX security.

6.4.1   Multics

*Multi*plexed *I*nformation and *C*omputing *S*ervice (Multics). Yes, the system that caused UNIX to be created because it was too complicated and the consortium needed an operating system that did one thing very well. Actually, one thing Multics did *really* well was security. It became the source of the *Orange Book*. If you look at Multics, you see what is needed for a security system.

1. *Hardware*. Multics ran on hardware (General Electric's GECOS and, later, Honeywell) that implemented memory protection in 36-bit segments. Each segment had 36-bit offsets, which made a combination of 72-bits (a whole bunch of terabytes) of memory. All computer storage (processor storage, RAM) and files were contained

inside the 72-bit area. All instructions were memory-to-memory. Protection was implemented in segment chunks and enforced by the hardware.

2. *Software*. The Multics operating system implemented a hierarchical security system.

   a. Access lists (ACCLS) allowed the systems administrator to designate lists of people who could access segments.

   b. Protection rings (similar to IBM System/360 protection keys) separated processes based on their level. Users were allowed to access information in the ring based on their level of authorization. They moved from ring to ring through a controlled entry and exit called a *gate* (similar to MVS and VSE supervisor calls and VM's diagnose functions).

      (1) Ring zero was the operating system.

      (2) Rings 1, 2, 3, and 4 were used by the operating system.

      (3) Ring 5 was used by most general users.

      (4) Rings 6 and 7 were not really used.

3. *Security was part of the architecture*. You didn't have to add anything to the system. It was built in.

If Multics was so great, why isn't it running all our computers today? Multics didn't last because it was resistant to tuning. All accesses were to a large area and demand paging became a bottleneck. Since there were no input/output operations as such, the I/O subsystem couldn't be tuned. Having the best security (or the best of anything) does not guarantee success. Whatever it is, it must be cost-effective.

Warning *If you can measure it, you can manage it! If you can't manage it, it goes away.*

6.4.2 MVS

MVS was not designed to be secure in the early days. (Surprise!) It grew from a batch computing environment (OS/MVT) that did not have much need for security. The data center was self contained and did no networking, and most of the data was on magnetic tapes so it was not available interactively.

As far as security goes, early MVS systems were identical to early UNIX systems. Physical security was all that was needed or desired because all the computing power and data was secure inside one or more rooms.

As MVS grew and interconnection to the data became more important to companies, the need for security grew. A password facility was implemented (for use by batch jobs and Time Sharing Option (TSO) terminal users). Unfortunately, the password file could not be shared between multiple systems. If you changed your password on one system, you had to change it on all other systems you needed to access because the password file could not be changed. (One of my earliest modifications to MVS was to make the password file shared between multiple copies of MVS.) Additionally, the file did not have the password encrypted. You could edit the file and learn all the passwords!

Today, MVS has centralized, uniform, enterprisewide security provided by the Resource Access Control Facility (RACF). It can be configured to qualify for a B1 security rating. (Maybe MVS could qualify as an A-level system, but nobody could tell anybody about it because that would be a security violation!) RACF, which IBM introduced in the early 1980s, provides multiple-system support, encrypted passwords, security rule enforcement, and the capability to implement security at the highest levels. The best thing IBM did was to develop exits or macros to call the security services. These documented, complete interfaces are now called *application program interfaces*

(APIs) and are generally entered via the RACHECK (macro) interface.

Shortly after RACF hit the streets, other vendors started building competing products. These products use IBM's API to build components the data center can use in place of RACF (ACF/2 and Top Secret are two of them). One term for these is *original equipment manufacturer (OEM)* products. The mainframe operating system has a large number of places for which non-IBM vendors can develop products, so it comes as a surprise that some people in the industry do not see mainframe operating systems as "open."

For many years, competing products ran head-to-head with RACF and were far superior to IBM's mainframe security system. Today, however, I see that most companies are using RACF, as it has been improved in the forge of competition.

Figure 6-1 shows a RACF implementation. At the top, two MVS systems are pictured. USER1 is operating on MVS1; USER2 is operating on MVS2. When these two users logged onto the operating system (TSO), the logon programs transferred control to the system RACF routines and the user ID and passwords were looked up in the primary RACF data set (SYS1.RACF.PRIMARY).

A backup data set is usually allocated in case something happens to the primary data set. The backup is made equal to the primary at initialization; all updates are made to both data sets.

Data access is controlled by specifying data set security. At the bottom of the figure is a payroll data set. Security can be specifically set (PAYROLL.WHO), generically set (all data sets that begin with PAYROLL), or not set at all.

6

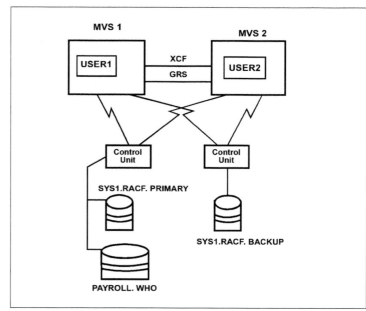

Figure 6-1. MVS RACF

RACF data sets are shared by all connected systems. In this figure, the DASD data set is SYS1.RACF.PRIMARY. Usually the data center keeps a backup data set in case the primary one is damaged.

Figure 6-2 shows how RACF works.

①A user or a batch job asks for a program to be run.

②An online teleprocessing monitor (OLTP) or the Job Entry System (JES) starts the task.

③The application program starts running.

④The program issues an open (part of open/close, end of volume). A supervisor call (or branch entry) jumps into MVS (similar to Multics's access lists).

⑤MVS passes control to the RACF routines (RACHECK macro) to verify if the user is authorized to access the resource or data set.

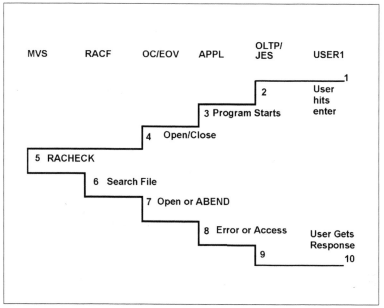

Figure 6-2. MVS RACF Checking

RACF is invoked at either logon time (JES) for user ID access, Open/Close/End of Volume (OCEOV) for data set access, or by the application as it checks for authority to perform some function.

⑥RACF looks up the resource and the user ID and passes back either an "OK" or a "failure."

⑦Open/close continues (unless the task was abended by a security failure).

⑧The application can now access the resource.

⑨The OLTP or JES subsystem passes the results back to the user.

⑩ The user gets his data.

In MVS 5.x running in a parallel sysplex environment, RACF uses the parallel coupling facility to access security definitions. One benefit of parallel sysplex (with MVS 5.1 and later releases such as OS/390) is that the hardware can notify a system when a record changes. As of this writing, neither RACF nor any other security system that I know of cuts off a user if his access changes after approval has been granted, but before the user is finished with the access. Take the case of a TSO user logging on and starting to access the payroll file with a stolen ID. Suppose someone finds out and cancels the ID. As long as the interloper does not log off (or close the file), he still has the stolen rights. Transmogrify into the future where RACF on MVS2 is instructed by the systems administrator to revoke the ID. MVS1 is notified (as it is today), but now RACF has been changed to look for the user and forces him off. Neat!

Some sophisticated systems (such as Landmark's TMON line of products) use RACHECK services to validate parts of their programs. For example, with **The Monitor** for MVS, the user can free common storage from the system common areas — very powerful! The prudent systems programmer would not want just anyone displaying information to have this capability (one can crash the system if one is not careful), so the systems programmer can set up groups of user IDs that have the capability; no one else will be able to access the commands.

Even applications you write can use the RACHECK service. For example, you could write CICS applications that display data only if a person's identification allows access. One usage is to allow anyone in the company to look into the payroll file and display a person's name and phone number, but allow only managers and human resource people to look at salaries and evaluations.

Most of today's database systems allow this type of restriction on access to information within a file. For example, DB2 allows you to protect tables with RACF groups.

6.4.3 UNIX

UNIX codesigner Dennis Ritchie once said, "UNIX was not designed from the start to be secure. It was designed with the necessary characteristics to make security serviceable." Keeping that in mind, think back to Chapter 1. UNIX was developed as a system that could do one thing really well. Designed by MIT and GE in the 1960s, it became operational relatively soon (as compared to Multics) because its focus was simply on running programs. Multics, on the other hand, concentrated on multiple functions.

Although UNIX was designed with a single major function in mind, it has several strong built-in security measures. First, by nature of its multitasking environment, UNIX prevents users or programs from interfering with one another and crashing a system. Aside from this common-sense measure, UNIX also contains inherent user controls that affect the access and privileges users have to the system.

So why is UNIX often dubbed a "nonsecure" operating system? The answer has three parts. The first is *programming*. All it takes is one flaw in a program to compromise an entire UNIX system. Notice the keyword here: one flaw in a *program*. Most UNIX security problems result from errors in programs, not the UNIX system itself.

The second part is generically called *trusted users*. Until recently, security was not an important consideration to UNIX users or designers. Since the primary users of UNIX systems (those in the academic arena and the computer industry) disliked security and viewed it as a needless hassle for so long, UNIX vendors harbored similar attitudes. It made sense to view the purpose of the product as the customer did: to make the customer happy.

6

The third part and biggest problem is that UNIX networks do not have *encryption capabilities*. Anyone who has access to the data flowing over the network (as *all* TCP/IP communication allows since all packets go to all nodes) has access to the data and, therefore, to the passwords and data.

One of the biggest problems with implementing UNIX security is that it is a distributed operating system.

Diversity often is rooted in complexity. Many UNIX systems administrators allow users to have a single networkwide login. The authentication process is handled by other UNIX systems and the user ID is passed onto other systems — a dangerous practice for systems that have business-critical applications. If you must use it, allow only those systems under your direct control to authenticate users.

Let's look at the MVS and UNIX security components. Remember, I am not trying to make you a security expert, just trying to familiarize you with the language of each so when you are in meetings with one or both disciplines, you can translate.

6.5 Security Components

In both the MVS and UNIX worlds, different components make up a secure system. Some are physical or external (like locked doors and rooms, locks and keys for individual systems, cardkeys, or devices that read fingerprints), while others are logical or internal (information stored in special files, for example).

6.5.1 The Security File

The security file is a logical security component that contains all of the information necessary to provide security for your system.

6.5.1.1 MVS Security Files

MVS uses a number of locations to store or from which to communicate security information: the RACF security file, SYS1.RACF (the actual name may vary); the systems measurement facility (SMF) file; the MVS (or other system) console; and the data security monitor. A typical MVS RACF security system is shown in Figure 6-3.

SYS1.RACF   The RACF security file (SYS1.RACF) is a direct access data set that can be shared by as many systems as have access to the physical disk pack for the file.

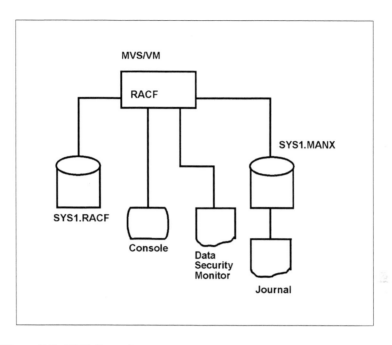

Figure 6-3. MVS Security

MVS (as well as VM and all other RACF-based systems) has a primary database (SYS1.RACF) and three other areas it sends dat to.

Access is controlled by using enqueue and dequeue system calls.

Console   RACF also sends messages to the systems console with a routing code to allow an organization to have a dedicated security console. Before automated operations packages, security officers may have had these messages printed on a printer in their office. Once I set one up for an internal auditor. He quickly tired of the clackity-clack and abandoned it for automated reports. With today's automated operations packages, you can even dial a beeper if a security violation occurs.

Data Security Monitor   RACF could be piped into the data security monitor for even more complete monitoring of possible security violations. Using this product, you can analyze incoming messages.

6

SYS1.MANX   The SMF files log information about user access.

Journal   The SMF processing system can build a journal of security information.

6.5.1.2   UNIX Security Files

UNIX has only one file that is used in security — the *etc/passwd* file — which is the basis of all security in UNIX. This file retains information about every user on the system, including:

- User name

- Password

- User's identification number and group identification number

- Full name of the user

- User's home directory

- User's shell (`/bin/csh`, for example).

A typical UNIX security system is shown in Figure 6-4.

If you view the `/etc/passwd` file, you see what appears to be a jumble of characters next to each username. This is actually a scrambled, or *encrypted*, version of the password. On some systems, however, passwords appear unencrypted in the `/etc/passwd` file, open to anyone with access to the file. To avoid this potential security risk, designers created an encryption algorithm that scrambles a password so that the encrypted password appears instead of the actual one.

6.5.2   User IDs

When a person accesses a computer system, we usually refer to them as a *user*. For example, I am Bob Johnson. I am also Robert Johnson. I am also Robert H. Johnson. I am also Robert H. Johnson Jr. Computers don't usually like blanks (actually, it is the programmers who don't like to parse out things with blanks!). They really don't like conversions from one name ("Bob") to other names (like "Robert"). Thus,

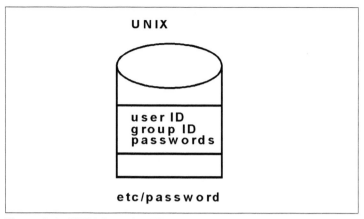

Figure 6-4. UNIX Security File

Standard UNIX uses a single password file to hold user IDs, group IDs, and passwords.

we create *user IDs*. These are handy identifiers for real people. If we had only developed some standards for user IDs, there wouldn't be so much confusion. Each operating environment has its own idea of what a user ID should look like. In most cases, an 8-character name with no blanks embedded will work.

6.5.2.1   RACF User IDs and Groups

RACF uses 8-character user IDs to control access. Each user ID has a set of attributes associated with it. Control can be granted to access files (through high-level indices) or pseudo groupings called *groups*.

Groups are logical entities in either system. I recommend you use groups unless there is no way to use groups to access a certain function. Take 10 people in Payroll. Add a high-level index (PAY1996) for a new-year's payroll system. Without groups, you would have to make 10 changes to the security database. If you have a group (such as *payroll*), you can add access rights to the group ("Let everyone create new data sets and write to them") and be done with it.

6

Want only two people to be able to create and delete data sets? (Never, never have just one person with the capability to manage a subsystem — when that person is gone, the requests will flow back downhill to you!) Create a group (such as *paymake*) with rights to create and delete data sets.

6.5.2.2   UNIX Users and Groups

In UNIX, all users have user names as well as *user identifiers (UIDs)*. UIDs are numbers that help the system identify a user. UIDs often range from -32768 to 32767, but sometimes range from 0 to 65535; the UID of 0 is reserved for the superuser. UNIX considers users with the same UID to be the same user.

Similar to the UID is the *group identifier (GID)*, which is another number that appears after the UID in the `/etc/passwd` file. This number indicates what primary group a user is assigned to. A listing of all groups and their members can be obtained by viewing the `/etc/group` file.

Unlike UIDs, GIDs should have more than one person assigned to them. Groups allow certain information to be viewed by several select people. If a group is assigned the same number, all users in the group have access to the same information. Users on this system who have different GIDs do not have access to the same information.

6.5.3   Special User and Superuser

How are operating systems configured? Who, if anyone, has the power to access all files on a system? What if you forget your password? These all-powerful users have the entire system at their fingertips. In RACF, they are *special*. In UNIX, they are *super*.

6.5.3.1   RACF Special User

The RACF user ID with the *special* attribute can do anything to any RACF record. Explicit access must still be given to certain entities, but the RACF special user can assign the ability to himself. For example, if Payroll was in a special group, the RACF special user could not read or write to the data sets but he could grant himself access to the data set.

6.5.3.2   UNIX Superuser

The UNIX *superuser* is a special user that exists in the root account, usually with a user name of *root*. You also can gain superuser status by using the su command. If you specify a login name, it will change your user ID and ask for a password. If you do not specify a login name, your privileges will be converted to superuser.

This special user is often referred to as *root user*. UNIX uses the root account to perform important functions such as I/O management (see Chapter 5) and keeping track of active and inactive users.

The superuser has significantly more power than a typical user. UNIX system administrators are often given this authority because they need to perform low-level tasks, often for general system administration. Normal security measures that apply to regular users do not apply to the superuser.

Table 6-1 summarizes the multitude of tasks a superuser can perform.

Table 6-1. Superuser Privileges	
Type of Control	**Specific Abilities**
Process Control	Can change a process's *nice* value (get or lose service from the CPU), signal any process, turn accounting on and off, bypass login restrictions prior to shutdowns, and become any other user on system.
Device Control	Has access to any working device; can shut down the computer, set the date and time, and read or modify any memory location.

6

Table 6-1. Superuser Privileges	
Type of Control	**Specific Abilities**
Network Control	Can run network services on "trusted" ports, reconfigure the network, and enter "promiscuous" mode and view all packets. Network access is one of the most vulnerable areas of security. If you can get to it, you can destroy it.
Filesystem Control	Can read, alter, and delete any file or program on the system; add, remove, or change user accounts.

It is important to note that the superuser is not omnipotent. Superusers cannot, for example, alter read-only file systems (unless they become the owning user). Because the superuser is not subject to normal UNIX security restrictions, the mere existence of the superuser is a threat to system security. If an outsider enters a system and logs in as a superuser, the resulting damage can be catastrophic.

6.5.3.3   To Keep You Out of Trouble

I recommend that all special/superusers use your special user ID only when actually performing security functions. You should have a "regular" user ID to use for all day-to-day functions and a "special" user ID for your security responsibilities.

Warning   *In other words, if you are using the* su *command without a login name or if you are logging in as root, then you are doing it all wrong.*

If you follow my recommendation, you may inadvertently access a protected file or function, but you will not hurt it. Yes, it will be uncomfortable to switch user IDs to perform security functions, but it will be safer. If you have to switch too often (more than, say, once a day), your security is not set up correctly.

Figure 6-5 shows one way (from **The Monitor** for UNIX) you can look at users to see if anyone has root authority. This is from a development machine with way too many "root" users. Don't have your machine look like this one!

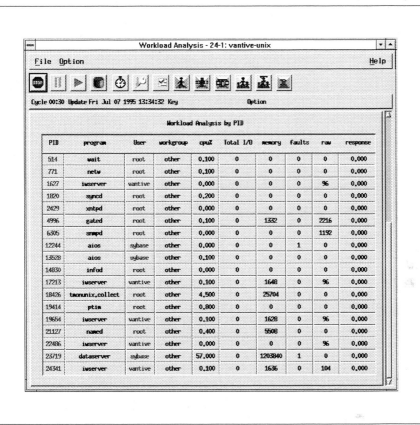

Figure 6-5. Who Is On Your System?

The Monitor for UNIX displays users on the system. You may want to use this display to see who is using your system from time to time.

6

6.5.4   Passwords

Passwords are your friends. They exist so you can authenticate who you and other users are. Without them, anyone can enter your user name and, if no other physical security measures (for example, a cardkey) prohibit them, wreak havoc on your system or view confidential files. Think of passwords as any operating system's second layer of security (physical

access or network access being the first layer). More
importantly, it is the one you control.

6.5.4.1 Passwords on Mainframe Systems

Mainframe systems using RACF or an equivalent
subsystem require a unique 1- to 8-character user ID
and a password of up to eight alphanumeric
characters. All uppercase letters, all lowercase letters,
or a mixture is treated as if the characters were
entered as all uppercase. Thus, user ID *william* is
identical to *WILLIAM*.

6.5.4.2 Passwords on UNIX Systems

To log into UNIX, a user must enter a unique 1- to
8-character, case-sensitive, user name, followed by a
password of up to eight characters. In UNIX, a
correctly entered user name and password
authenticates the user and grants access to the system.
Group settings determine exactly what files a user has
access to.

6.5.4.3 Protecting Your Passwords

Passwords are the most vulnerable of all security
items. After all, the key to the kingdom is the
password. Once the door is opened, whatever lies
behind the door is available tot he person in the door
jamb.

A password should be known by only you and your
system. Let me say that again,

Warning *A password should be known by only you and your
system.*

Let me put that into perspective for you. What if one
of your worst nightmares came true: A person finds
your driver's license and speeds from town to town,
collecting speeding tickets in your name? You turn up
to renew your license, and they throw *you* in jail. You
would probably be mad! If you don't give your
driver's license (or checkbook or credit cards) to

anyone, why would you want to give out your user ID and password?

Poorly selected passwords — for example, a birth date, your spouse's name, or the name of a pet or child — are one of the leading reasons for security breaches on UNIX systems. Hackers, or *crackers*, as they are sometimes called, try these obvious choices first when attempting to break into a legitimate user's account.

Another problem area is systems that automate logging onto your system(s). If you place your password into a system so it can automatically log you onto a remote system, a lot of things can happen, all of them bad.

For example, someone can steal your systems (or just its files) and log on as you. I have seen friends build elaborate scripts on their laptop computers to log onto their systems, pull down information, and log out. It may seem like a good idea until someone steals your laptop, because now they have your system, your data (you *are* backing up your laptop, aren't you?), and access to all of your systems — phone numbers, user IDs, passwords. And they are probably using your phone credit card number!

Warning *Change the distributed maintenance passwords for each of the software products you bring into your system. Most secure software systems (even the operating system) come with a startup ID and a password for their version of the special user or superuser. Ensure that passwords distributed with systems are changed after you install the system and before you open it up to others.*

One mainframe operating system is distributed with the user ID and password for a special user so the systems programmer can get started. The user ID must be provided by your vendor for startup. Tales of this user ID being left active are so rampant that I won't even go into them. Smart, cunning, or just evil people try the combination and get into the system

6

with full powers. If a systems person leaves this ID and password unchanged, they are just as liable as if they left the retail store door open, the cash register unlocked, and all the receipts in the drawer.

6.5.4.4 Setting Your Password

Regardless of the system you are using, you can develop a process for creating your passwords that keeps them safe, yet allows you to access your systems. Never have a password that is in the dictionary. Programs are written to try every word in the dictionary as a possible password. Try this process:

1. Create a base for your password (3-4 characters that are not easily deciphered by people who know you).

2. Add a suffix of 1-4 alphanumeric characters that you change periodically.

3. Try never to write down your password anywhere, or at least never write down the complete combination in one place. For example, you may have the first item above written in your wallet and pick a pattern you can replicate (number of months-old your child is, not the birthday).

6.5.5 Data/File Security

The real pot of gold on your system is your data files (unless the attacker is just a pervert). After user IDs and passwords, the next area to concentrate on is what access is provided to what data files.

6.5.5.1 MVS File Security

MVS file security is based on the data set name. MVS data set names can be up to 44 characters long broken into 8-byte segments separated by periods (for example, *PAYROLL.1996.RAISE*. Note that the name is in all uppercase letters).

DASD Files   The MVS architecture defines many file types, including sequential, partitioned, and Virtual Storage Access Method (VSAM). MVS files are all treated alike. The security is either applied at open time or by an intelligent application.

Tape Files   Tape files are always sequential in nature. One file is built by writing to the tape drive. When the whole file has been written and is closed, the rest of the tape can be used to store one or more other files. There is no index on the front of the tape. If you are looking for a particular file, you must scan the whole tape. All tapes have a logical end-of-tape indicator (two tape marks) to prematurely stop searches.

6.5.5.2   UNIX File Security

The file system acts as the police force, of sorts, for UNIX security. It facilitates the allocation of secondary memory for efficient storage and retrieval of data. File systems control who has access to what data.

Files and File Permissions   In Chapter 5, you learned that UNIX views everything as a file. UNIX stores general information about files, such as size and type, as part of its file system. UNIX also retains information about the file (UID) and group (GID) owners. *File permissions* enable you to review the access privileges of other users on the system regarding particular files.

You can use the `ls -l` command to bring up information about the access privileges of the owner and group (and even others not in the group) as well as the file type. Users are allowed to read (indicated by an "r"), write ("w"), or execute ("x") a file, or any combination of these three activities.

File permissions are an important facet of security on the UNIX system. If you "own" a file, you can control who has access to it. Superusers have the ultimate power because they are able to change the file permissions of any user or file.

6

**Directory
Permissions**

Just like everything else, directories are viewed as files by UNIX. Thus, they, too, have owners, groups, and permissions. The only difference between directories and other files is that UNIX treats the levels of permission differently with directories.

Without execute (x) permission, a user is unable to determine the length of files or the file UID or to change to a directory to make it the current directory. Also, without authority for a directory, a user is unable to access files in that directory even if that user owns them.

Device Files

Device files are created by UNIX when peripherals, such as a printer or a tape drive, are attached to a system. Perhaps you have guessed that since very few computers run independent of peripheral devices, especially in the workplace, there are usually many device files on a UNIX system.

Device files can be a potential security risk. All device files are stored in the /dev directory. Users should not have the ability to read or write to most of these files. Resourceful invaders change their permissions, get into these device files, and use them to alter their access privileges, UIDs, or GIDs, giving them great power where they shouldn't have access at all.

**Tapes and
Other Offline
Data**

Tapes and other forms of data, often stored off-site in the event of a fire or other disaster that could destroy on-site records, present another level of security concern for UNIX users. Tapes and disks are, for example, physically separate from the online data and contain old records from which valuable information can be obtained should they fall into the wrong hands. Aside from a lock and key or similar measures, there is no way to protect this data.

All operating systems have trouble securing tape files. The problem is that the tape media can and often are apart from the security system that is trying to protect the data. About the only way to protect a tape is to encrypt the data on the tape.

6.6 Encryption Systems

Encryption means transforming a data element (message, field, or password) called *plaintext* into another form called *ciphertext* by operating on the element mathematically with a special encryption password called the *key*. Most use the same key when converting the plaintext to the ciphertext and back into plaintext. If you give the conversion routine the wrong key, you will get back garbage.

Encryption is the only method that allows you to have your data *in the open* for others to see. You can see that your data is vulnerable before and after it has been encrypted. The data can still be changed by the attacker if the goal is to destroy the transmission, not to find out what is in the transmission.

Unfortunately, many encryption routines have *back doors* or additional ways by which an encrypted file can be decrypted by someone without knowing the key. For example, many years ago there was a database system called *System/2000* (or System 2K). In a data center where I worked at the time, the database administrator lost the encryption key and, along with it, all of the data. We called the company and, lo and behold, the guru recovered the data. In my early years, I was naive: I was thrilled at such a wonderful solution. Then I began to think about the ramifications. This guy could get into any System 2K data set. I don't know if they ever closed that back door, but I would sure ask, in writing, what my database vendor has to say about back doors.

Your worries will never end. One public domain security system for UNIX and personal computers has had the federal agencies openly demanding to have a back door installed so they can intercept and decipher "criminal activities." This, too, sounds like a good idea until you think about it.

6

6.6.1   Types of Encryption Systems

There are two major types of encryption systems: private keys and public keys.

6.6.1.1   Private Keys

Private key systems use the same key to encrypt and decrypt the data element. Table 6-2 lists the private keys.

Table 6-2. Private Keys	
Name	**Description**
ROT13	A simple substitution algorithm. It probably is the most widely used encryption in UNIX for mail systems and other general purpose "keep it from most eyes" tasks. Don't depend on it.
crypt	Another simple algorithm (it was the basis for mechanical encryption machines).
Data Encryption Standard (DES)	Bingo. DES is a bit permutation, substitution, and recombination function performed on blocks of 64 bits of data and 56 bits of key. DES is the basis of the mainframe's RACF security system. As of this writing, there are no standard UNIX programs that perform DES encryption. You may want to find some UNIX source. Many implementations of DES now use hardware to encrypt and decrypt data elements.

6.6.1.2   Public Keys

Public key systems use one key to encrypt and one to decrypt. The name is derived from the fact that you can make one of the keys public without compromising the secrecy of the message or the other key. Table 6-3 lists the public keys.

Table 6-3. Public Keys

Name	Description
Privacy-Enhanced Mail (PEM) or RSA (named after the inventors Rivest, Shamir, and Adleman)	This system uses two cryptographic keys, a *public* key (to encrypt a message) and a *secret* key (to decrypt it). It is more of a programming toolkit than a security system.
Pretty Good Privacy (PGP)	PGP was developed by Phil Zimmerman as a protest for free expression and test implementation of secure digital signature technology. It is supported on most UNIX systems as well as desktop systems. It is the most popular of the public key tools.

6.7 Networks and Security

Even if a company has spent plenty of money on security, employs many technicians well-versed in security measures, and trusts all of its employees, security can still be at risk. The problem may not come from *within*, but from *without*.

Networking provides nearly limitless opportunity for information gathering. That is why Al Gore was completely wrong when, during 1992-94, he was urging us to keep from having *information-haves* and *information-have-nots*. Everyone is already an information-have. Information is only good when it is converted into data, then into knowledge. It then becomes empowering. Only when you reach *wisdom* will you excel. The government rarely helps us to knowledge, much less wisdom.

Illegal access affords unauthorized users to capture or damage data. There are ways to help secure a network.

6.7.1 The Physical Network

Large groups of computers linked together via modems are becoming more and more common. On a network, such as the Internet, you can send and

6

obtain a wealth of information from the comfort of your own desk.

The Internet configuration is not much different than an interoffice network configuration, such as a LAN. Users have IDs and networks have addresses. But, while the security threat exists with any LAN, it is much more obvious a concern with the Internet simply because so many more people are using Internet.

There are several components to every network, including the Internet, that need closer inspection.

6.7.1.1   Modems

Modems (modulator/demodulator) are devices that let us communicate with others and download information over distances. Users on the Internet send mail to one another and can download data using their modems. Often, the modem is viewed only as an asset to computing because of its ease-of-use, speed, and remarkable capabilities.

Unfortunately, modems also can work against us. You can communicate with others and download their information; others can communicate with you and download, even alter, *your* information, whether you want them to or not, in some situations. Your modem must be in answer mode, but it can happen.

Securing your modem lines is now, more than any other time in the past, an integral part of security. By allowing your modem phone numbers to be known to as few people as possible, you reduce the risk of an unauthorized user tampering with your system via modem. Also, maintaining one modem for outgoing calls and a separate one for incoming calls can be a successful deterrent to hackers. This tactic prevents them from gaining access to systems through a combination outgoing/incoming line and being able to dial into a system and download data using that line.

Warning *One of the most dangerous aspects of a modem is that access to your system is across phone lines and in the form of audio signals. Think about the following scenario. You are in your hotel room writing a politically damaging article about people in high places. When you are finished, you log onto your company's system and upload the article. It is late, about midnight, so you sign off and go to sleep. At 3 a.m., your article is slipped under your hotel room door with threats written on the paper. Scary? It happened.*

What if you were in a hotel room and built a bid for a very large and important project for your company and shipped it off to your boss only to have your numbers diverted to your competition so they could underbid you? As of this writing, the cellular phone people are struggling with phone identifications being intercepted and used by hundreds of other "roaming" phones.

6.7.1.2   UUCP

Like all UNIX networking code, UNIX-to-UNIX Copy system (UUCP) was not part of the original UNIX design; it was added later. UUCP is a group of commands, programs, and files that allows UNIX users to network with one another over a dedicated line or a telephone line. Modems used in conjunction with UUCP enable users to extend their network to *Usenet*, an electronic bulletin board system consisting of many special interest groups.

The security dangers of such a configuration are obvious. With all those people out there communicating and exchanging information, there is a possibility that someone could enter your system and alter or copy data.

Table 6-4 outlines some of the measures UUCP provides that help prevent security violations. These steps have proven effective in minimizing the security risks of UUCP.

6

Table 6-4. UUCP Security Measures		
Security Concern	**Mechanism to Prevent Unauthorized Use**	**Reason**
Unauthorized login	Assign password to UUCP account to prevent unauthorized login.	uucico program must log into your system to copy files and run commands.
A user is able to read information in a secure file	uucp **user can read only spooled** UUCP **files and files that are readable by every user.**	uucp programs do not run SUID root, but SUID uucp.
UUCP login receives a normal shell	Only system administrator-issued functions can be performed.	Normal shell is not received. Instead, a copy of uucico is activated.

System administrators, it should be pointed out, do have more power than the typical UUCP user. For example, a system administrator has the ability to allow remote users to retrieve files from selected directories only.

6.7.2   Network Services

UNIX networks have a number of indigenous services built into them. Table 6-5 describes some of these services and the security risks associated with them.

Table 6-5. Network Services Security Risks		
Service	**Function**	**Security Risk**
Electronic Mail (E-Mail)	Enables users to send and receive messages.	Messages containing privileged information can be intercepted.
File Transfer Protocol (FTP)	Enables transfer of files between systems.	Password required for entering remote system could be intercepted and used for unauthorized logins.

Table 6-5. Network Services Security Risks

Service	Function	Security Risk
Finger	Yields detailed information about system users by scanning /etc/passwd file.	If service is not disabled, then anyone can use it. Information available on local machines is also available to network users who enter this command.
rexec	Enables user to execute remote commands.	Password must be transmitted over network, subject to interception by unauthorized user.
TELNET	Enables network users to log into remote computer.	Similar to modem risks: unauthorized user can obtain remote access to your computer.
Trivial File Transfer Protocol (TFTP)	Simple program that allows workstation booting over the network.	Little or no security provided. Will transmit certain files to any computer that asks for them.
X Window System	Enables multiple programs to share the same graphical display.	Any network client connected to X Window Server gains complete control of display.

6.7.3 Commerce on the Internet

Even as I write this, the trade journals are full of articles on how businesses will be and are using the Internet for commerce.

One of the things often said about networks is "Don't use your credit card over a public network." I, for sure, would not because the pain of someone getting my credit card and using it for thousands of dollars of stuff they bought is just too great! (Yes, I know there are limits to our liability, but just working with multinational companies is a pain!) Anyway, I want to run up my own credit card bills for useless stuff!

6

Having said that, there will be commercial protections for using credit cards over the network. Let's look at a scenario of how that might happen.

1. A customer sees a product he'd like to purchase and sends his PGP public key and phone number to the company's sales department.

2. The company calls the customer, verifies his user's key, and transmits the company's public key to the customer.

3. The customer fills out an order form, adds his credit card number, and sends the file to the company.

4. The company decrypts the file, processes the order, and charges the customer's account.

The credit card number is never transmitted in raw form. EDS, MCI, and others are forming a consortium of organizations to allow distributed credit card sales. Watch those spaces!

6.8 Add-On UNIX System Security

ennis Ritchie's assertion from earlier that UNIX has the "necessary characteristics to make security serviceable." We have discussed its built-in measures for security; now it is time to discuss add-on devices that can improve UNIX security.

6.8.1 Kerberos

Kerberos is an add-on authentication system spawned from work MIT, IBM, and Digital Equipment Corporation conducted in the early 1980s. It encrypts sensitive information so it cannot be easily intercepted or viewed by unauthorized users. Though not much different than running "regular" UNIX, Kerberos requires significant modifications to existing system software.

6.8.2   Secure RPC

Sun Microsystems' Secure RPC also is an add-on authenticator for UNIX systems. It is different from Kerberos in the way it encrypts information for transfer over a network. Secure RPC can be used only with certain SunNet products.

6.8.3   Firewall Machines

Actual firewalls are constructed to slow the spread of fire from one building to another. Likewise, *firewall machines* slow or stop the progress of invaders on a system. The two parts of a firewall, the *gate* and *choke*, divide the outside network from the internal one. The *gate* and *choke* can be configured in a number of ways; you can specify what information is transferred in and out of your system.

6.9   Threats to Security

No system is immune to security problems. Current employees, disgruntled former employees, and outsiders have been known to compromise supposedly secure systems. This section describes, in general terms, additional threats to systems.

6.9.1   MVS and the SVC

In the early days of MVS, when a systems programmer or vendor wanted to implement a program that performed tasks requiring supervisor-level authority, we just wrote a supervisor call (SVC) routine and called the SVC from our program. The first 128 SVC numbers (zero to 127) were reserved for IBM routines and the last 128 (128 to 255) were reserved for local and vendor numbers. In most cases, the installation started at the highest number first. Thus the SVC *255 syndrome.*

Being naive, we merely set the program into supervisor state and returned to the calling program. The problem was that anyone knowing the SVC number could get *their* programs into super mode

6

(since we all started with 255, guess which one you would start your search with?).

This loophole is mostly covered by awareness in the data processing industry. Most vendors don't even use SVCs anymore to install their software. Landmark has completed the conversion with the latest releases of their MVS platform monitors. In some cases, the vendor (or facility programming staff) can't avoid SVCs, but they should be written in such a manner that they cannot be compromised easily.

6.9.2   UNIX

One of the most publicized threats to security on UNIX systems came when a young man, Robert Morris Jr., wrote a UNIX-based Trojan horse.[1] The term *Trojan horse* is used as it was in ancient Greece: something "intended to defeat or subvert from within" (from *Webster's Ninth New Collegiate Dictionary, 1986*.) In this case, it was a program written to contain other programs that gained control and did things the end user did not request. In the PC world, these are know as *viruses* because they are small, but wreak havoc!

Another, less publicized case, but one much more worthy of your consideration, involved the escapades of Clifford Stoll outlined in his book, *The Cuckoo's Egg* (Doubleday, ISBN 0-385-24946-2). Cliff is the genius who discovered foreign espionage agents accessing the Arpanet/Milnet/Tymnet connections. I recommend this book to anyone with an interest or responsibility in the area of security of systems software.

But enough already about other systems problems and solutions. What about your situation?

---

1   Mr. Morris was a Cornell University graduate. In November 1988, he transmitted a program designed to break into UNIX through a series of design flaws in the program. His program worked too well and disabled a large number of UNIX computers around the world. He was sentenced to three years probation in April 1990.

As outlined earlier in this chapter, UNIX has a wonderful file system protection scheme. But its strengths also are its weaknesses. If any program uses the *SETUID* bit to obtain root permission, any user can assume root authority. Just like SVC 255 in the MVS mainframe environment, this can be a compromising situation.

Besides the Trojan horse described above, numerous other "menaces" to UNIX system security exist. These are outlined Table 6-6. Some may be familiar to PC users.

Table 6-6. Threats to UNIX Security

Threat	Description	Best Ways to Protect Against Threat
Viruses	Alter programs on computers they enter and, like true viruses, insert copies of themselves that spread damage throughout your system or network.	Protect all /bin directories, do not use questionable code on your machines, and ensure that only you have the ability to write to your directories.
Trap Doors or Back Doors	Allow access without usual authentication procedures. Trap doors and back doors are bits of code that allow quick access to the program.	Remove all back doors/trap doors from program after debugging is complete, check important files regularly, and thoroughly understand program source code.
Logic Bombs	"Wait" until certain conditions are met within a program, then "detonate," causing damage to the system or the system to halt.	Thoroughly understand program source code.
Worms	Move from computer to computer and can cause damage, but they do not change the programs they enter. Worms *can* carry other threats that do change programs, such as a Trojan horse.	Ensure the system is as secure as possible against unauthorized user access.

6

Table 6-6. Threats to UNIX Security		
Threat	**Description**	**Best Ways to Protect Against Threat**
Bacteria	Make copies of themselves in a system. Can overwhelm system resources and make them unavailable to users.	Do not use questionable code on your machines and ensure that only you have the ability to write to your directories.

6.9.3   Government Intervention

Probably the largest threat to security is by the United States Government and the logical grouping called *clipper chip*. Throughout the last several years, the government has held onto a proposal that would mandate that security systems built in the United States **contain a back door with a super-user key that is available to law enforcement agencies.**

Sounds like a neat idea: Make it hard for criminals to encrypt things. The idea comes from wiretaping. The government could obtain judicial approval to tap the voice communication of a suspect and thereby gain evidence on potential wrongdoing. Unfortunately, in the world of electronics, capturing information being passed around the network is incredibly easy. Anyone can do it. With or without judicial approval. You don't need the telephone company. You don't need special approval. All you need is this single super key. Want to make a bet it will not be in the wrong hands?

A number of organizations are providing information and clarification. One is *Wired Magazine* (www.wired.com). Another is the Center for Democracy and Technology (www.cdt.org). If you are in the security business, you should use the web to keep up to date.

6.10 Summary

Security is a decision. Security is a corporate policy.
It is not a technical consideration because security
costs money and you get what you pay for.

Always be vigilant with your system security and
make frequent backups of your system. Both of these
steps will minimize the damage and down time your
system may suffer should an unauthorized user ever
gain access to it.

6

Chapter 7: Tuning I/O in MVS and UNIX

The most interesting and profitable area of tuning is the I/O system, including the hardware involved. It has never been more interesting or profitable than at this time in history. Manufacturers have discovered what performance analysts have known for years: "I/O is the problem!" Most studies say that 80% of performance problems are related to I/O response problems. Mainframe, distributed, and desktop manufacturers create hundreds and thousands of improvements each year addressing I/O problems.

Today, even the school child is likely to know that IDE drives are different from SCSI drives! My 4-year-old granddaughter knows how to "undo" a math program to bring back the aquarium. "Load it from disk."

Tuning I/O may seem like trying to document the path of a straw hat in a hurricane! There are so many I/O operations going on, what is important? But we have been here before in the mainframe environment and learned that you *can* tune I/O. Let's look at some basics and then you can use these concepts to help you understand your distributed or PC hat as it flies by!

7.1 What is Systems Tuning?

It is pretty obvious that mainframe folks know systems tuning. It's a whole industry! But when these folks get over to UNIX, they discover that each system is completely different from any other system. There are no standard measurement metrics and logging of performance management data is strictly a do-it-yourself process. In fact, there seems to be no *tune* in UNIX. Well, *PerformanceWorks* /SmartAgents for UNIX (the new name for Landmark's TMON for UNIX) puts the *tune* into UNIX. You could almost call it *TMON the Tuner* (a take-off on StarKist's Charlie the Tuna®, which provides quality in canned tuna fish like TMON provides quality in performance tuning!).

7

Tuning systems is a very broad topic that can be broken down into three parts — processing power (CPU), shared processor storage, and I/O components (our threesome from Chapters 3, 4, and 5!). *Processing* and *storage* in our two environments are managed by finding out who is using the resource and fixing the system so that the "loved ones" get the resources and others wait if necessary.

The third, and most important, area of tuning is the *input/output subsystem* (MVS) or *file system* (UNIX). You can do the most good or the most harm to your end users by meddling in the I/O subsystem. I believe the more things change, the more they are alike.

Solving any performance-related problem requires first that you detect it. So the story goes with disk I/O problems in both the MVS and UNIX environments. But how do you know you have a disk I/O problem? For that matter, how do you know you have any problem? Your first indication might be when the phone rings. What's worse is that the caller won't say, "You have a disk problem!" They will say something like "Response to my xyz database is bad." Chances are you won't know much about the database. But you better know your system and how to detect problems on it.

7.2 Tuning Mainframe Hardware

Tuning MVS covers volumes and volumes of information. Most of it is aimed at the things you can do with software parameters (such as the MVS SRM parameter files). I believe the place to start, *before* you turn those tuning knobs, is the hardware. Even most mainframe systems managers don't realize that you need to look at the hardware configuration before you begin to tune the operating system. You would be surprised at the number of configurations I have seen that have only one path to DASD (usually because the four or eight paths must be allocated to logical partitions (LPARs)).

7.2.1   The Overall Plan

First, try to draw your configuration on paper. This is hard to do because you must find out how things are connected under the floor or logically. Usually you will find that the hardware vendor who provides your mainframe has the most accurate and up-to-date map.

Next, you must apply an understanding of the volumes and the data on the volumes. (Just what you will have to do when you get to tuning UNIX.)

Then start asking what happens when an I/O goes to a database. Do you see all of the production volumes attached to a single control unit? ("It was the cache controller.")

Keep your diagrams because they will be very useful when you get to the real performance problems in MVS: I/O problems.

7.2.2   Connectivity

When you were trying to draw your configuration, you undoubtedly noticed that all I/O devices are connected to the processor complex through channels and control units. Channels are inside the processor complex and control units are external to the processor complex in a separate box. Today, control units have more raw processing power and more cache storage than most processor complexes of just a few years ago. Channel and control unit knowledge is vital to all who are interested in making their I/O operations (and, therefore, their applications) operate in the most effective manner.

Figure 7-1 shows a typical mainframe/MVS configuration. A channel is an integral part of the System/370 architecture, like the slot and its supporting electronics in a PC. Channels and slots serve similar functions in their respective architectures. Instead of a slot into which an adapter card is inserted, a channel terminates in a connector at the bottom of the processor complex. Instead of an

7

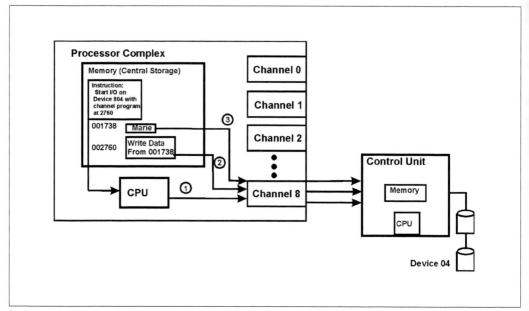

Figure 7-1. I/O Operations in MVS

When the CPU executes (at ①) a START I/O instruction (for System/370) or a START SUBCHANNEL (for Extended Architecture, or ESA, systems), the instruction gives a device identifier and channel program address to the control unit. The control unit fetches the channel program instructions (at ②) and data (at ③) from central storage through the channel.

adapter card, there is a control unit located in another box.

The channel and control unit are connected with copper (electrical BUS and TAG) or fiber optic (ESCON) cables; one end plugs into the processor complex, the other into the control unit. You cannot, of course, plug BUS and TAG cables into optical fiber channels or vice versa.

Think of these cables as extension cords that carry control and data signals between the two. The control unit and I/O devices are connected with similar (though different) cables, much as I/O devices are connected using cables to adapter cards in a PC or SCSI in UNIX boxes.

A channel in a processor complex can have any type of control unit plugged into it. The software inside the processor complex must be told what type of control unit is plugged into which channel, but the electronics do not care.

Each control unit, like each adapter card in a PC, is designed to work with a particular type of I/O device. You cannot, however, plug a direct access storage device into a tape drive controller. On most distributed (or PC) systems, you can plug all kinds of units into the same "channel".

There are portions of the electronics and CPU inside the processor complex that permit software to control and respond to I/O devices using the channels and control units. The CPU has general-purpose I/O instructions, controllers can access central storage without the simultaneous attention of the software, and there are facilities to interrupt what the CPU is doing and cause it to do something else.

7.2.3   Processor Complex to I/O Device

The I/O instructions in a processor complex specify an address that, in turn, specifies the channel, control unit, and device. Let's look at these parts.

7.2.3.1   Channel Paths

In Figure 7-2, you see a schematic representation of a loosely coupled system: two processor complexes, a control unit, and an I/O device are shown as boxes, and the cables connecting them are shown as lines. A set of I/O devices connected to a controller is called a *string*.

Note that the third box down inside the processor complex is labeled "Channels/Directors." In mainframe processor complexes, the connection electronics are called a *channel*. In the 3033 processor complex, channels were combined into *directors*, but that name was eliminated when the 3880 control unit was developed with directors.

7

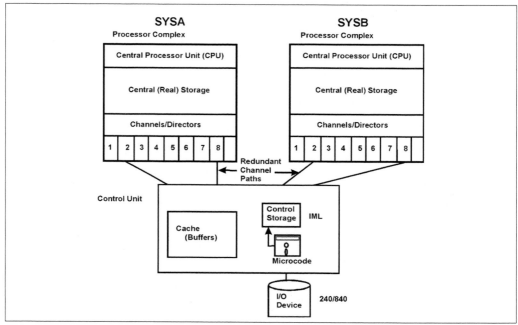

Figure 7-2. I/O in Mainframe Environments

The mainframe channel architecture performs the same basic functions as a desktop or distributed architecture, but does so from more than one CPU inside a processor complex or from multiple processor complexes. The reason is that I/O devices are configured externally from the ability to process instructions. The above logical presentation shows two processor complexes accessing a single storage control unit.

Channels and devices, including I/O devices, are numbered for identification. The combination of a channel and an I/O device number is usually called a *device address*. In the case of DASD, this address is used by the software to identify a particular actuator.

Control units also have a unique, 2-digit number, which is usually seen only in console messages about the control unit.

But must a control unit be connected only to a single channel? It depends on the particular model of the control unit. Must a control unit be connected only to a single processor complex? Again, it depends on the control unit. In Figure 7-2, Channels 2 and 8 are connected.

Also in Figure 7-2, a single control unit and its attached devices are connected to two processor complexes. The processor complex on the left can access the control unit and its devices using Channels 2 and 8. That processor complex may be running MVS, VM, VSE, or any of the System/370 or System/390 operating systems.

The processor complex on the right also can use Channels 2 and 8 to access the same control unit and devices. That processor complex also may be running any of the System/370 operating systems, but not necessarily the same operating system as the processor complex on the left.

Although the same channel addresses are used on both processor complexes, they need not be. For example, the control unit could be connected to Channels 2 and 8 on one processor complex but to 3 and 7 on the other. That would be confusing to a system operator since a device would be known as 240 (alternate path 840) on SYSA and the same device would be known as 340 (optional path 740) on SYSB. The reason we use the same channels on both is to minimize confusion, not only in the example but also in real life. This permits us to identify the box that is the control unit by its channel address or addresses without further qualification. It also helps to have the channel numbers the same on two processor complexes when one may be used to take over for the other in the case of a primary CPU failure.

In the following, then, when we say *Channel 2*, we mean the channel inside the processor complex with the control unit attached to it. Also, when we say *access a device*, we mean *access a device through its control unit*.

Channels 2 and 8 are redundant channel paths: They provide two ways to access the same data on each processor complex. Most data centers configure this way intentionally to get *performance* and *availability* advantages:

7

- *Performance* is enhanced by taking advantage of parallel I/O operations for two or more devices. *Redundant channels do not help access to a single device* but they do enhance operations for more than one device on a channel. This is a mainframe advantage, because in the UNIX SCSI arrangement, one device can lock out all other devices on the channel. It is also why the mainframe has much wider bandwidth for I/O operations.

- *Availability* is enhanced by having redundant channel paths to the same control unit: If one path becomes unavailable, the data is available through the other.

The System/370 architecture allows I/O operations to proceed simultaneously if they are on different I/O devices and channels. A channel requires some time (albeit small) to initiate and service an I/O operation. If *channel busy* time becomes a bottleneck, this constraint can be relieved by splitting the load among two or more channels.

Not only is performance enhanced, but the system can tolerate some kinds of component failure. In the example, the operating system can access a device through both Channels 2 and 8. If either of these channels becomes *broken* or *unavailable* for some reason, the end users can still access their data if the control unit and device remain functional.

What is one way a channel could be unavailable but not broken? If the processor complex were physically partitioned (for example, 3084 physically partitioned or PR/SM), with Channel 2 in one partition and Channel 8 in the other, and the operating system in one partition failed, users could access their data through the other partition.

There are two other kinds of redundancy that data centers may employ for the same reasons as channel redundancy. First, redundant controllers can be used with some DASD models. In this case, if one controller fails, the other can be used; the two controllers share the I/O load with each other. I highly recommend two control units (or two power-separated sides) for each string of DASD.

Second, redundant DASD can be used for enhanced availability. One way to do this is with *dual copy* (a feature of 3990 control units), in which each I/O write operation is performed simultaneously on two different actuators. If one actuator fails or its data becomes corrupt, the data is available on the intact device. I recommend this feature only for very valuable data because the cost of implementing dual copy is relatively high. UNIX and LAN systems refer to dual copy as *mirroring*.

Note   *Dual copy on the mainframe could be compared to mirroring in distributed environments but it is simpler to implement. Many manufacturers suggest you have mirroring on all your disks (a great way to sell hardware!). For the mainframe, dual copy is implemented as part of the control unit. The control unit processor is doing the work, not the processor working on your task/processes. In all non-mainframe processors, mirroring is accomplished from within the processor. It steals cycles from the CPU you are using for your applications. One distributed installation told me that they reduced their CPU utilization by half (and thereby made their applications run twice as fast) by eliminating mirroring. You may need the safety of dual copy or mirroring, but there is no free lunch! Be careful.*

After the mainframe hardware is tuned, you must turn to buffer tuning either in the task itself or in the database manager. The best I/O is one satisfied by moving data from one central storage buffer to another. There are too many options for buffering I/O blocks in the mainframe environment to cover them here. They are very important to understand and implement.

7

You must get the hardware right first because eventually the program must get its data from the external devices. Think of hardware tuning like the old story of the young child who was bugging his father while the father was reading *MVS Concepts and Facilities* (a shameless plug). The father took a page from a magazine that showed the earth from space. You remember, it looks like a big blue and white marble. The father cut the picture into lots of little pieces and challenged the child to put it together. Thinking he now had lots of time, the father returned to the book. A few short minutes later, the child returned with the picture put back together. "How did you do that so fast, the earth is all blue and white swirling lines?" The child said: "There was a picture of a man on the other side. When I got the man put together right, the world was, too."

When you get the hardware put together right, you can get the I/O tuning done.

7.3 Tuning UNIX

Like the mainframe, tuning UNIX is a repetitive task. Unlike a circular task, where you would do the same things over and over, tuning must start somewhere and the next step is based on what you found in the current step. One of the first steps to take is looking at the hardware and the operating system. Evaluate what you have and be sure it is configured properly.

The second step is to run `defrag`[1] on all of the disks. (This works as a second step for mainframe, distributed, and PCs because in all likelihood no one has run defrag at all. It is super-important for distributed and desktop systems.)

---

[1]   The term *defrag* here refers to the UNIX command to combine portions of a file that are not in contiguous spots on a spindle into a single, contiguous number of disk sectors. On the mainfame, Innovation Data's FDRABR or IBM's DFHSM have similar functions. On the PC, it is usually a disk utility such as PDISK.

The third step is to balance the file systems. Most UNIX systems attach devices via the *small computer system interface (SCSI)*. (PCs also use the SCSI interface in addition to the IDE interface. SCSI is better, but that is another story.)

If you are looking at a small system with only one SCSI channel, your only hardware-tuning option is to move data sets from volume to volume. If you are having I/O response problems on a small system, you should probably add a second SCSI subsystem and balance I/O requests over the two paths.

If you are looking at a large system or one with networked connections, you can move data sets from channel to channel or system to system. Let's begin at the beginning: the hardware.

7.3.1 Accessing Local Data

The primary difference between mainframe and UNIX systems is that, on the mainframe, I/O to local devices is standardized by the principles of operation and the original equipment manufacturing interface (OEMI) specifications and UNIX implements I/O operations as a loadable option. Performance analysis of a centralized system uses a mature set of performance tools with understood metrics. The result is a clear understanding of which resources are being used, by whom, to what extent, when, and what for.

Devices attached locally to a UNIX system can be (and usually are) proprietary architectures, even at the interface level. [Yes, mainframes are beginning to get solid-state devices and RAID equipment attached that are based on SCSI, but the control units are *plug compatible* to the OEMI.] Client/server in general (and UNIX in particular) makes everything more complex.

As a mainframe person, I started thinking that UNIX I/O was like mainframe I/O. **How wrong I was!** Instead of having the application (task) start the I/O and control it from beginning to end (a single procedure), UNIX **has four distinct subsystems**

7

acting asynchronously: the system call interface, the I/O subsystem, the device driver interface, and the hardware (SCSI controllers, cables, and devices). The definitive word here is *asynchronously.* Figure 7-3 shows the relationships.

7.3.1.1   System Call Interface

At the top of Figure 7-3 (outside the box) are the processes accessing data. These processes want to read and write data. They do so via a system call into the kernel code to access their data. Remember, in distributed programming, programs are written completely independent of the input or output device.

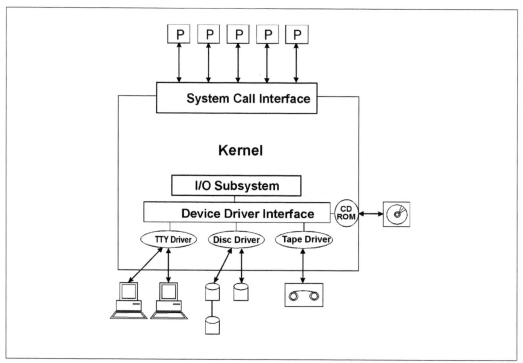

Figure 7-3. Four Phases of UNIX I/O Operations

UNIX I/O operations have four phases to them. The system call interface is used by processes (P). The I/O subsystem, part of the kernel, takes the request and hands it off to the device driver interface. Wires and devices complete the I/O architecture. Each has its own systems management characteristics to consider.

Straddling the top of Figure 7-3, the system call interface takes the process requests and either gets their data from buffers or goes to the kernel subroutines to get the data. Even the system call is isolated from other environments.

Note that the system call interface straddles the line, half in the kernel and half out in the user arena. The open/close/get/put code is partially in the program itself and partially a branch. In the mainframe, such code also is partially in the program (BALR RE,RF) and partially in shared memory such as PLPA.

7.3.1.2   I/O Subsystem

Another part of the kernel, the I/O subsystem, takes care of access control, buffering, and device naming. The I/O subsystem views devices as high-level abstractions.

Figure 7-4 shows a logical representation. The input to the I/O subsystem is buffer requests from the system call interface. The output is calls to the device driver to fill the buffers.

Now you see the confusion for mainframe programmers. On mainframes, the *I/O subsystem* is the code in the nucleus that handles input/output interrupts and schedules things on the channels. For UNIX, it is just a buffer scheduler and interrupt handler.

The kernel keeps a buffer structure for control of the request very similar to the input/output block (IOB) in MVS (addresses of routines, block number, bytes transferred). The difference is that the kernel builds and maintains the block, not the application or its data management services routines. This buf structure is passed to the device driver to fill buffers.

7.3.1.3   Device Driver Interface

The device driver accepts buffer requests from the I/O subsystem and handles the interface to the devices

7

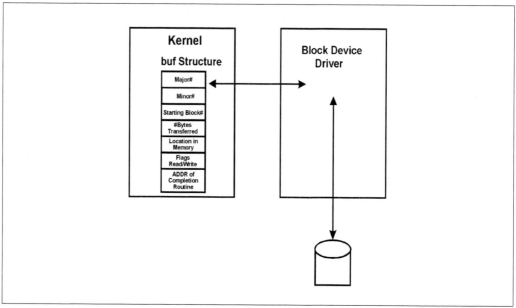

Figure 7-4. UNIX Kernel Operations for I/O Operations

The UNIX kernel buf structure has the same types of things that the MVS input/output block (IOB) structure has. For example it contains the pointers to buffers and the byte count for operations. These are passed to the block device driver for the real I/O operation.

themselves. This is more like the mainframe input/output supervisor. Devices *interrupt* the kernel and the kernel passes control to the interrupt handler described for a device (similar to the *first-level interrupt handler* on the mainframe).

The device driver interface calls the individual drivers. Drivers are provided by the hardware or software vendor and are plugged into the kernel at boot time. Thus, in the figure, you can add a CD/ROM drive, new tape drivers, or new disc drivers at any time.

7.3.1.4 Wires and Devices

The fourth area of concern when studying I/O interaction in the distributed environment is the wires and external devices. In most cases, a SCSI interface is used for this purpose. SCSI is such a large topic, I have dedicated Appendix B to the SCSI hardware and software environment, but a few aspects are important to this I/O tuning discussion.

Figure 7-5 shows the request-based access that usually occurs on a SCSI interface.

① A request comes from a device driver and is passed to the hardware card.

② In this example, the request is a read-data request for Disk 1.

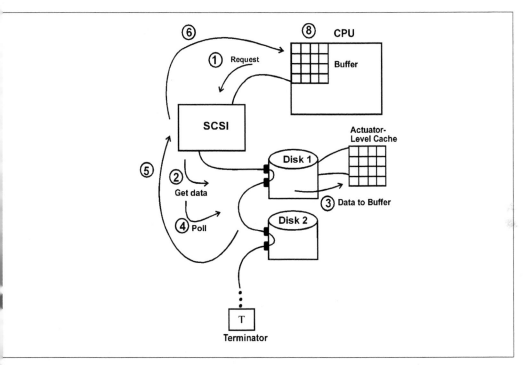

Figure 7-5. SCSI Operations

SCSI operations are usually a polling type operation. At ① above, a read request for disk1 comes from the CPU. At ②, the disk is asked to read the data, but the disk record is not in the cache. While the disk is reading the record at ③, the SCSI operation continues to poll other devices (at ④). Only on another polling cycle is data transferred (at ⑤).

7

③ The device may have the data in an actuator-level cache or it may have to read the data from the spinning disk into cache to be passed back to the requestor.

④ In any case, the SCSI protocol goes on to poll other devices.

⑤ This continues until all devices have been polled.

⑥ When the entire loop is completed, the process returns to the CPU with data or looking for other requests. Note that the CPU must have a number and it may be 0, 1, or 8. The number is always the "highest priority" number (usually zero) because the CPU always has priority for service.

You can see that such round-robin access lends itself to blockages and performance problems. For this reason, be sure you have ample "cache" so data buffers are available as they are needed or there may be a long wait for data.

Speaking of the term "cache", there are quite a few caches in this diagram. Cache is another term for buffers. All modern CPUs contain buffers for the instructions and data that are operating at any point in time. The SCSI card and the spindle or actuator usually have buffers to store data as it is being transferred.

7.3.2 Accessing Remote Data

In UNIX, a file system may be mounted (like the mainframe `mount`, making it available to users) as if it were local (attached to this processor), but really exist at some UNIX system feet or miles away. This is a neat implementation, but presents performance analysts with quite a challenge to understand and manage.

To gain a simple understanding of the scope of the problem, let's examine the two common implementation choices: accessing data as files and accessing data via a service.

7.3.2.1   Accessing Data as Files

The first technique for accessing remote data is through a *distributed file system*. Client machines can be configured to transparently access remote files as if they were local. Using a distributed file system, you can centralize file storage (that is, store files on a small number of servers), yet access the files in a distributed manner. Figure 7-6 shows one example of this implementation, the Network File System (NFS).

NFS was introduced by Sun Microsystems and is a very popular implementation that is available on platforms from PC to mainframe. Fortunately, Sun made the specifications available to all and now it is common on most UNIX platforms. Novell's Netware

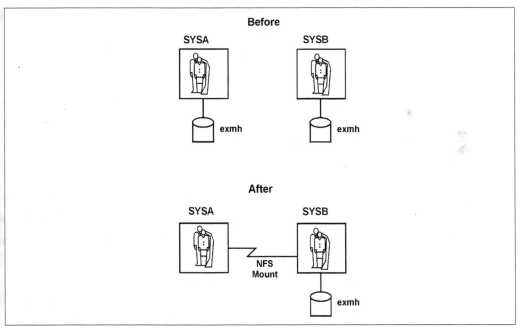

Figure 7-6. NFS Programming

In the top figure, each system has a copy of the exmh *program. In the figure at the bottom, the systems administrator has only one copy of the program and is nfs-mounting the drive (on SYSB) to the system on the left (SYSA).*

7

is another very popular implementation for PCs and low-end servers.

In the figure, at the top, the shareware program exmh is on each system. Below it, a shareware directory is established and shared by both systems. This is very appealing to most administrators because there is only one place to maintain software. If you are using exmh from SYSB, you will not see any difference. If you are on SYSA, you may see slower access if the network is bogged down. You may even be the cause of the network slowdown.

Unlike on the mainframe, the "shared storage" is not at the end of a channel cable, but at the end of a network connection. Networks get bogged down much faster than channels with large data flows because networks are designed to pass small packets of data to and fro. Willard Scott and Ed Walker, local Washington, DC, radio personalities, had a theme song many years ago that went something like: "We are the joy boys of Radio, we chase electrons to and fro." You don't want your customers to sing: "We are your disgruntled users, we chase our data blocks to and fro" (around the network).

7.3.2.2   Accessing Data via a Service

The second remote-access technique is to use a *service* or *interface*. Remote databases provide data to clients requesting information using SQL statements. Clients use a vendor's proprietary front-end application or a toolkit or library to build custom front-ends that communicate with a database back-end process that has local access to the database. This interface layer performs the data communications required to contact the server.

When developing applications, you can use either standard mechanisms such as remote procedure calls or a message-queuing service or proprietary protocols to create a distributed application.

7.3.2.3 Tuning Implications

In all of these cases, the I/O service time is dependent on the responsiveness of the remote system. Your application needs a data block, so it starts a request. The actual I/O to the device to get a physical block may leave your operating system and go across the network, into another (maybe different) operating system and wait on its I/O subsystem. (See the "Andrew File System (AFS)" for a discussion on ways to improve this.) Great fun!

There are some standard UNIX commands (for example, `nfsstat`) that can give you information, but you probably will have to monitor the remote system to see what is really happening out there.

7.3.3 Application Considerations

Like the mainframe, the applications programmer really controls the calls for data and system services. This means that, sometimes, the applications programmer also can have performance problems.

7.3.3.1 When It Takes a Long Time

One of the problems with remote files is that the updates to the real file system pointers are updated when the file is closed.

In Figure 7-7, you see a local-cloned system with two records being updated with three more records. When the file is closed by the program, the file system must update all of the pointers on the remote system. For a few records, this may not take much time. For several hundred records, this may take a long time.

7.3.3.2 When Data Disappears

Another problem concerns the sloppy programmer. While loss of data may not seem to be a performance problem, I feel it is the ultimate performance problem. How long does it take you to read a file that is gone? Forever. As the old saying goes: *On an empty disk, you can seek forever!* If the programmer eliminates the application close, the file may not get updated until

7

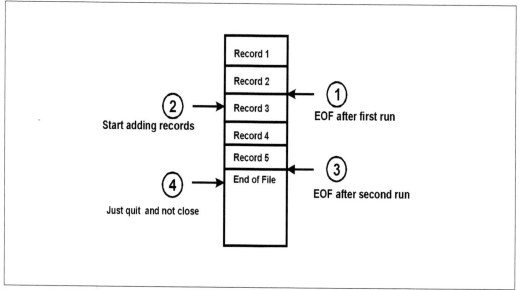

Figure 7-7. UNIX Applications Considerations

UNIX applications programmers may see unusual problems if the files are not closed properly. In this case, the program wrote two records and closed the file (at ①). It then started adding records (at ②: record 3) but it just quit or the system crashed after it wrote record 5. Either the file will still appear to have only two records, or the end of the program will take a long time (I have seen minutes!) to end.

the file system detects a problem (open?). Ever hear of data being mysteriously lost?

Continuing with Figure 7-7, suppose the three records were added, but the programmer did not close the file and the operating system/data base did not detect this and update the pointers to show the additional records. Now you have "lost" records.

7.3.4   UNIX Metrics

I/O metrics in UNIX are usually gathered by using the `iostat` or `sar` commands. UNIX commands have a funny attribute: They report the counters since the last boot (IPL for mainframe folks). That is REALLY a great number to have (NOT!). I learned this and went to my UNIX system and typed in `iostat` to see what happened. I did it again, thinking that the numbers would be since the last execution of the command. Well, that is when I learned that `iostat` does not clear the counters in the kernel, it only reports them. To get what I wanted, I had to issue `iostat 300 12` to get 12 reports (one every five minutes) and then I had to throw away the first report.

Note   *Monitoring is a disruptive business. One of the tenets of performance monitoring is to do no harm to the system while measuring (like in medicine, the doctor wants to do no further harm to the patient). Think carefully before you set any monitor for less than five minutes. The process of collecting the data may adversely affect the system you are trying to monitor.*

A sample report from `iostat` is shown below. Note that the second through fourth lines contain the values since the last boot. You should throw them away.

```
Disks:      % tm_act      Kbps      tps      Kb_read    Kb_wrtn

hdisk0        0.0          0.0      0.0        3324        0

hdisk1        0.2          1.0      0.2       61817      79576

hdisk2        0.5          2.4      0.4      116596     218720


hdisk0        0.0          0.0      0.0          0         0

hdisk1        0.0          0.0      0.0          0         0

hdisk2        1.0          3.9      1.0          4         0
```

The values received are:

% tm_act. Indicates the percentage of time the physical disk was active (bandwidth utilization for the drive).

kbps. Reserved to indicate the average kilobytes per seek. This field is left blank for physical disks that do not make this data available to the system.

tps. Indicates the number of transfers per second that were issued to the physical disk. A *transfer* is an I/O request to the physical disk. Multiple logical requests can be combined into a single I/O

7

request to the disk. A transfer is of indeterminate size.

Kb_read. The total number of kilobytes read.

Kb_wrtn. The total number of kilobytes written.

7.3.4.1   The Monitor for UNIX Metrics

One way to see if you have a problem with your hardware configuration is to look at the way devices react under your load. Figure 7-8 shows a sample **The Monitor** for UNIX report. Each device is

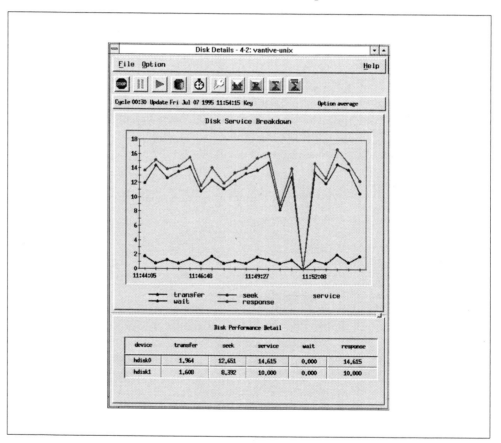

Figure 7-8. The Monitor for UNIX Disk Details Report

The Monitor for UNIX displays information in graphical mode (for example, at the top the response time) and in tabular mode (part of the devices are shown).

displayed as a line graph and a table of actual values. Both styles of display are required for you to gain the most from the display. Note the table at the bottom shows raw numbers. It would be very difficult for you to spot the clear dip at 11:52, yet that clearly is a time when something out of the ordinary happened.

The table of actual numbers is vital for you to understand the metrics for multiple devices because the scale of one might hide problems with others. For example, if *hdisk0* was normally 70 kbps, then the fact that device *hdisk1* went to zero at the same time would be hidden in the graphic display. Be aware that if one device is doing a large number (sorry I can't define "large" because 10 I/Os per second could be large on one system and 20 I/Os per second small on another), it might be masking problems on other devices.

7.4 Summary

Tuning I/O operations begins with the hardware and then follows a path back to the application. Each operating system is different, yet each has the same components. Programs ask for data and the operating system provides it. In order to tune these systems, you must be part detective, part hardware expert. Most of all, you must be determined to understand how the process works so you can make changes and have them improve the performance, not have things stay the same or get worse.

7

Appendix A: Translation Dictionary

The premise of this book is that common terms or concepts exist between UNIX and the mainframe operating environments. The first section of this translation dictionary is sorted by mainframe terms with a UNIX equivalent given where applicable. A UNIX-to-mainframe section is provided later in this appendx.

This appendix is not intended to provide a complete glossary of terms for either platform. The Xephon *Handbook of IBM Terminology* (Xephon: Lewisville, Texas 1-817-455-7050) or the IBM *Dictionary of Computing* (SC20-1699 or later replacement) are excellent primary sources.

Mainframe to UNIX

ASID table
A table in the MVS operating system storage that contains pointers to the address spaces active in the system. Each MVS address space is assigned a sequential identifier from 1 through 32768. The UNIX equivalent is the *process table.* Each UNIX process is assigned a *process ID (PID)* number from 0 through 29,999.

attach
The MVS mainframe software allows a program to ask to start another unit of work for a specific task. That may be to take advantage of parallel processing (in a multiprocessor) or to wait for a specific event (wait for an I/O operation to complete). The UNIX equivalent is *spawn.*

C
A letter in the alphabet or the hexadecimal letter used to represent 12 in a base 16 numbering system. For the mainframe, "C" is the name of the language that represents the source code for many UNIX operatives. There are many versions of the C compiler. SAS Institute markets a mainframe compiler and is at least

partially used for most of its products. See "UNIX to Mainframe," later in this appendix, for a UNIX-only description.

cache

Another term for a buffer that usually describes proprietary random access memory (RAM) in a piece of hardware. In mainframe systems, *cache* is most often used for RAM in channel control units. The term *high-speed buffer* usually is used instead of *cache* in the central processor.

capture ratio

The percentage of CPU time the operating system can attribute to tasks running under the operating system. The missing parts are CPU spent on behalf of the system or some task that can't be identified at the time the CPU instructions are being executed. As an example, take an I/O interrupt. Any task in the system could call for an I/O to be performed. When the I/O is completed, the channel subsystem interrupts the processor and the operating system stores the status, handles any error condition, does housekeeping for the I/O first-level interrupt handler, and then notifies the task. Only the last part is usually charged to the requesting task. The first parts are uncaptured and go into a timer bucket as "overhead." In MVS, the capture ratio is usually in the 80% range.

common storage

MVS common storage (such as CSA or SQA, or VM shared segments) is used by tasks to read and write information available to all address spaces under the control of the operating system. The UNIX version is the *shared memory segment.*

CPU

Central processing unit. The definition of CPU in the mainframe environment is identical to its definition in other environments. It is the part of the computer that performs (or executes) instructions. The more CPUs you have, the more likely the mainframe operating systems will satisfy your users. Under the covers, however, the I/O subsystem, the logical partitions,

A

and other "computer" functions may be running on a "CPU" that has another name in the hardware diagram.

cursor-select

The mainframe, using 3270 devices, implements item selection by placing the cursor on a certain spot or column and hitting the ENTER key. In the distributed or desktop world, this is called *drill down*.

DASD

Direct access storage device is the term used in the mainframe environment as the equivalent to *spindle* or *disk* in the UNIX environment.

disk

The mainframe literature refers to the spindle of spinning platters as a *disk*. UNIX refers to the same hardware item as a *disc*.

IPL

Initial Program Load. The mainframe term for starting the operating system. It is usually performed after a *power-on reset* of the hardware. The UNIX equivalent is *boot*.

ISPF

Interactive System Productivity Facility. A user interface to the operating system running under a terminal control program (TSO/TMP or VM) that uses 3270 protocol. (A terminal user also could be using the TSO CLIST processor or the REXX command processor, or even something like Super-Wilbur!) The UNIX equivalent is the *shell*, only there are many versions (C-shell, Bourne-shell, etc.). Another UNIX equivalent might be the open management platforms (OMP) such as Sun, OpenVision, and NetView for AIX. ISPF is coming to MVS: Open Edition for MVS has an *oispf* command to run ISPF under the POSIX-compliant UNIX running under MVS.

job

Equivalent to the *batch process* in UNIX. In either case, the work is performed without waiting for or writing directly to a person at a terminal.

multiprocessing

In the mainframe environment, more than one CPU is available to the operating system and any task can be dispatched on any of the available CPUs. As open systems evolve, there are two types of multiprocessing. *Asymmetric multiprocessing* means that more than one CPU is available but CPUs are dedicated to a specific task, such as disk or network I/O. *Symmetric multiprocessing* means that more than one CPU is available to all of the processes performing computing functions. These CPUs usually share I/O and memory. The same concepts are true in UNIX.

MVS/ESA

Multiple Virtual Storage/Enterprise System Architecture. The name of the IBM operating system for mainframes. The UNIX equivalent is *UNIX*.

object code only

IBM, once upon a time, distributed both source code and object code to customers. Customers also were their competitors. In the early 1980s, IBM started shipping only the executable modules. Vendors of software running on the mainframe almost never shipped their source code. See *source code* in "UNIX to Mainframe," later in this appendix.

privileged mode

Programs that require the capability to execute powerful, operating system-like instructions (such as set program mask) are said to be in *privileged,* or *supervisor, mode.* The UNIX equivalent is *superuser mode.*

RJE

Remote job entry. When the mainframe is connected to another copy of MVS and users on the first copy route work to the other with a "/*ROUTE" job control language statement. The UNIX equivalent is the *task broker.*

SMF

MVS *Systems Management Facility.* Equivalent to the UNIX `sadc` data-collection program. SMF places data in SYS1.MANx files, which are copied to daily, weekly, monthly, and even annual files. Unlike `sadc`, SMF has a large number of record types and facilities to create or bypass record types.

started systems task

In MVS, an address space that runs independently of end-user control. UNIX refers to this as a *daemon process.*

SVC

Supervisor call. The name of a System/390 instruction that performs a state change from program mode to supervisor mode. The service requested requires systemwide authorization such as GETMAIN virtual storage or perform I/O operations. The UNIX equivalent is the *system call.*

task

The unit of work in MVS. The term used in UNIX systems is *process.*

TCB

Task control block. A field in storage that controls and monitors tasks. Each task has a *TCB.* The fields contain information about the program executing, the registers, and other information about interrupted tasks. UNIX has a similar block called the *process control block.*

TSO

Time Sharing Option. In MVS, the name given to the terminal control program. VM uses the term *Conversational Monitoring System* (CMS). UNIX uses the term *shell.*

UIC

Unreferenced interval count. The MVS variable used to monitor real storage page frames. The UNIX equivalent is the *lotsfree* page stealing variable and the *GPGSLO* tunable parameter.

VM/ESA

Virtual Machine/Enterprise Systems Architecture. This mainframe operating system is transaction intensive.

VSE/ESA

Virtual System Extended/Enterprise Systems Architecture. This batch and transaction mainframe operating system is designed for smaller, lower cost systems than those for which MVS is designed.

UNIX to Mainframe

A

This section of the dictionary provides UNIX terms and mainframe equivalents, where applicable.

asymmetric processing

See *multiprocessing* in "Mainframe to UNIX," earlier in this appendix.

batch process

Batch processes perform work in the UNIX environment without being associated directly with a person at a terminal. They are the MVS equivalent of a *batch job* and the VM equivalent of a disconnected virtual machine. UNIX users most often think of their non-terminal work as *disconnected* work rather than batch processing.

boot

The UNIX operating system is started by the *boot* process. A *warm boot* is associated with a command or switch on the processor that starts the process without turning the power off and on again. A *cold boot* is done by completely powering the processor off (to reset cards and peripherals) and back on again. The mainframe equivalent is the *Initial Program Load (IPL)*. The only mainframe equivalent to a warm boot is what systems programmers put on when they go skiing because their systems are running smoothly.

C

The C compiler is the source basis for the UNIX operating system. There are many versions of the C compiler. Standard extensions to UNIX are created by simply adding source material to the system libraries prior to system generation. The C"++" compiler is object oriented.

CPU

Central processing unit. In UNIX environments, CPU is used like the term is used in other non-mainframe environments. It is the part of the processor that performs (or executes) instructions. Multiprocessing (using more than one CPU to perform instructions) is relatively new to the UNIX environment, so multiple CPUs take on new meaning in the UNIX environment.

daemon process

A UNIX process that runs independently for various system functions, such as print spooling. The term *daemon* is sometimes pronounced like the word "demon," but more recently has been pronounced "dA-mon." Maybe it's the politically correct crowd again. The mainframe equivalent is *started systems task*.

disc

The same as direct access storage device (DASD) in the mainframe environment. Mainframe literature uses the spelling "disk." See also *spindle*.

disconnected process

See *batch process*.

drill down

To get to information about a certain field, you click or double-click on the field. This is called *cursor-select* on the mainframe.

kernel

The UNIX kernel is the operating system component that is first given control upon boot. Applications call routines in the kernel to perform storage, I/O, and CPU services. Mainframe equivalents are *MVS/ESA*, *VSE/ESA*, and *VM/ESA*. The kernel is the equivalent to the MVS base control program (BCP) and Data Facility Product (DFP).

lotsfree

The UNIX `lotsfree` page-stealing variable and the `GPGSLO` tunable parameter are used by the kernel to control paging. (There is a whole group of them besides these including `minfree` and `desfree`). The *unreferenced interval count (UIC)* is the mainframe variable used to monitor real storage page frames.

process

The smallest unit of work in UNIX. The mainframe equivalent is *task*.

process control block

UNIX kernel programs need a block to track processes
running in the system. This block is similar to the
mainframe *task control block.*

process ID (PID)

Each UNIX process is assigned a PID number from 0
through 29,999. The mainframe equivalent is *address
space identifier (ASID).*

process table

The kernel table of pointers to processes active in a
UNIX machine. The mainframe equivalent is the
ASID table although all operating systems maintain a
table of tasks to run.

sadc

The data collection program in UNIX that saves data
in directory /usr/adm/sa in files named sadd
where the "dd" should be the day of the month. Each
sadc file contains one record for each execution of
sadc. Thus, if sadc is run each 15 minutes, there will
be 96 records in the file. The equivalent to the UNIX
sadc program is the *MVS Systems Management Facility
(SMF)* or *VM accounting facility.*

shared memory segment

The area of virtual storage that is accessible to other
processes and their virtual storage. The MVS
equivalent is *common storage.*

shell

The terminal interpreter program that interfaces the
user to the operating system. There are a number of
them you may be using. The *C shell* (use the
/bin/csh command) is the base shell. The prompt
you will see is customized to the directory you are in
(similar to the pg command in PC DOS), probably
the percent (%) sign. The *Korn shell* (use the
/bin/ksh command) is another version; the prompt
is the number sign (#). The *Bourne shell* (use the
/bin/sh command) is still another version and the
prompt is the dollar sign ($). To see what version you
are using, type *echo $SHELL.* To change your login

default (across logouts) to the one in use, type *chsh*. The MVS equivalent is *TSO* and *ISPF*. The VM equivalent is *Conversational Monitor System (CMS)*, *ISPF*, or other terminal monitor.

SMP

Symmetric multiprocessing. UNIX computers may have more than one CPU. Each hardware manufacturer calls their multiprocessor configuration by a different name. SMP is one of those. In the mainframe environment, this is called *tightly coupled multiprocessing* (more than one task executing during the same machine cycle).

source code

Originally, the UNIX operating system was shipped only in source code, similar to mainframe source code ships. The mainframe has moved toward shipping object code only, which means that new releases of old products and almost all new products are shipped without the source code. For the vendor-specific versions of UNIX (for example, HP/UX, Sun Solaris, and IBM AIX), source code has never been shipped for two reasons: The vendor wants to maintain a competitive edge and does not want the source code modified in a way that will cause maintenance problems.

spawn

UNIX tasks may want to start units of work to either take advantage of multiprocessors or to provide a way to wait for an event without having the main task wait if it can be doing other useful work. Mainframe uses the term *multitasking* or *attach*.

spindle

UNIX uses the term *spindle* or *disc* to describe the direct access storage device. The mainframe uses the term *DASD* or disk.

superuser mode

To execute kernel or near-kernel operations, the process or user must be in this mode. The MVS (or other RACF system) equivalent to this is *privileged*, or *supervisor, mode*.

system call

A kernel call that requests services that require the operating system to perform privileged operations such as I/O operations. The MVS equivalent is the *supervisor call (SVC)*.

task broker

Usually associated with HP machines. A UNIX user can ship work to other clients. For example, if you want to do a compile or SAS procedure to manipulate large files, you can say, "Run this over there on Sam's machine." On the mainframe, you would ship jobs to other copies of MVS or other VM virtual machines and run *remote job entry*, or RJE. As you can see, this makes for interesting capacity planning exercises. Your client machine may be 100% busy while you are on vacation!

Appendix B: Small Computer System Interface (SCSI)

This appendix concentrates on locally attached, block-structured devices. UNIX devices can be divided into two categories: serial devices and block devices.

Serial devices are read from or written to in serial mode. The first block is read, then the second, and so forth. Serial devices are normally used by only one user at a time until the user is completely finished with the device. Most of the time, UNIX makes the serial device look like a single-file structure.

Block devices can be shared by a number of users. They usually are accessed through the UNIX file system, although certain processes can read from or write to them in *raw* mode.

Block devices also are called *disks* or *spindles*. Disks are used when the block device is a spinning platter and data is stored on the platter. Spindles are used to indicate that there may be a number of platters on a shaft. The collection of data on the platters is the *device*. Current implementations can be in solid state (RAM) or in Random Array of Inexpensive Disks (RAID). To minimize confusion, these devices are referred to here as *disks*.

Serial mode devices (tapes) are attached to small computer system interface (SCSI) channels, as you will see, but block-structured devices are the most interesting for the performance analyst. Most of your considerations will be for disks attached to servers you will be able to see and touch. Some file systems are actually on other servers and accessed remotely on a *network file system (NFS)*. Even if your problems involve remote disk access, the hardware is local to some machine, so let's start there. UNIX boxes must have properly configured hardware before you consider the software or tuning parameters.

Most UNIX hardware uses the SCSI interface to attach peripheral drives to the processor. Indeed, some tuning experts come into a UNIX situation and just reconfigure the hardware to fix *all* of the performance problems!

SCSI Types

There are many types of SCSI interfaces. You could almost say that each hardware implementation of an SCSI model is a different type. To begin to understand the types and your implementation of them, you will need to know a few terms. Table B-1 describes the terms.

Table B-1. SCSI Types	
Type	**Description**
Synchronous SCSI	The oldest type of SCSI that, as the name implies, processes requests as it gets them. They are attached with cables designed to carry eight bits of data at a time. This is usually called *SCSI-1* and was found on 1980-vintage computers.
Asynchronous SCSI	The type most hardware and software uses today.
Differential Signaling SCSI	In synchronous and asynchronous SCSI, the signal is carried on the wires at about five volts. For example, zero volts for a cycle would be a zero bit and a +5 volt signal would be a one bit. If the cable is affected by electrical noise, there might be errors that force a retransmission. Differential signaling generates a +5V and a -5V. Noise still affects the signal but the receiver is more likely to differentiate correctly. Differential signaling may increase the cable length to 25 meters.
Fast SCSI	As its name implies, this type of SCSI is designed to run at twice the rate of synchronous SCSIs (10 MB per second).
Wide SCSI	Transmits 16 bits of data rather than eight in each clock cycle. This doubles the data rate to 10 MB per second.

Table B-1. SCSI Types	
Type	**Description**
Fiber Channel SCSI	Fiber optics channel cables can be used to carry about 25 MB per second and can run up to 1,000 meters or more.
Tagged Command Queuing (TCQ) SCSI	Perhaps the most sophisticated and important type of SCSI. The buffer and optimizing occurs in the drive, not the controller, which allows the controller a large range of overlap options, including the ability to : • Process more than one I/O request to a drive at a time. The queued commands can be executed as soon as the current one is completed. • Executing commands out of order. Seek times, rotational latencies, or both can be minimized. This is a 2-edged sword. It is supported in Solaris 2 but not in SunOS 4. If you are trying to use TCQ in a mixed-device environment, you may find errors when it is in use.

B

Some hardware vendors combine the architectures, such as Fast-Wide SCSI. For example, the IBM 3590 tape drive is a SCSI-2, fast-wide, 20 MB/second device that attaches to a RS/6000 or power/parallel SP2 system. The devices search at 166 MB/second and can transfer 30 gigabytes in three minutes. The tape is 128-track metal tape, which (as of this writing) holds 10 GB uncompressed.

Warning   *Your biggest challenge will be to get the right cable for your SCSI configurations. On occasion, you might hear someone asking if anyone has a particular SCSI cable with the proper ends. It is not just the ends. Ensure that you get the cables that match your configuration. To be sure, you should probably order a spare to test for bad cabling and to add devices when necessary. Waiting weeks for the right cable is no fun.*

SCSI Configurations

Figure B-1 shows the basic SCSI configuration. The control unit is usually a card in the processor. It has attachments (shown here at the bottom) to one or more devices. Devices are numbered either from zero to six or one to seven. There always is one more device identified to the SCSI device and it is usually "eight," which is the CPU. It is not really a device but a card that must have an identification point. For the rest of this discussion, the devices will be 1-7 and the CPU will be 8.

The terminator is drawn in these figures with a separate box, but it is usually just a cable connector with no cable coming out of the end.

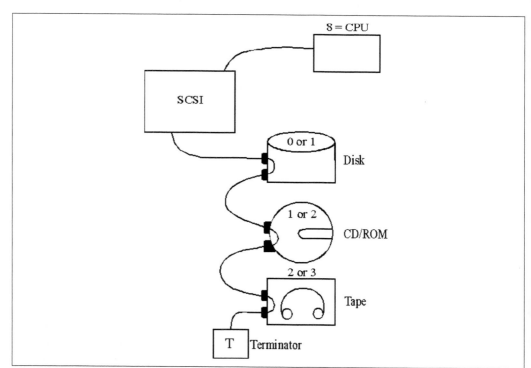

Figure B-1. Basic SCSI Configuration

SCSI is the small computer system interface designed to connect disks (spindles), CD/ROM drives, and tape drives to small computers. Connection is by a series of cables, ending with a terminator (it looks like the end of a cable without a cable).

Request Paths

Figure B-2 shows the request path for an I/O operation on a SCSI channel. The circled numbers give the sequence.

① An application on the processor asks for a read or write to a device.

② The SCSI control card converts the request to a device selection action. In this case, Device 1 is asked to read a block of data. The devices move the actuator arm and wait for the data to come

B

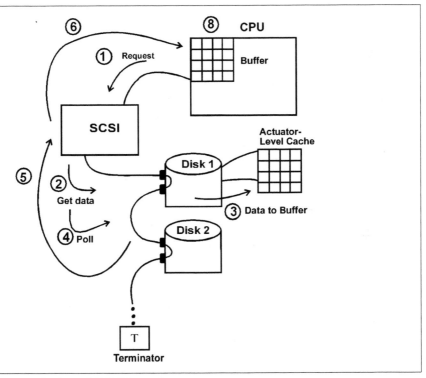

Figure B-2. I/O Request Path on SCSI Channel

SCSI is a polling architecture. In this figure the CPU (at ①) asks to read a block from disk 1 (at ②). The data is not in the actuator level cache, so the actuator starts the process (at ③) to move the arm, find the record, and read it into the buffer. The SCSI channel continues with other devices to see if they have any work to be performed. On another, later, cycle (at ⑤), the data is moved to the CPU (at ⑥).

under the read/write heads. Meanwhile, the SCSI controller goes on to the disk.

③ Most disk devices have a buffer, called *actuator-level cache*. This buffer is used to buffer the data from the spinning platter in anticipation of a read request. On writes, the buffer is used to store the data until the platter is positioned properly for the data block. (I often wonder why disk brakes are not installed to stop the platter immediately when a read or write is wanted to wait for the channels!)

④ Eventually the SCSI controller polls each device looking for work to do.

⑤ The SCSI probably has a buffer to store the data before it passes it onto the CPU.

⑥ When it is time for the CPU to be notified, the buffer will be transferred to the CPU buffer.

Polling

SCSI architecture is a round-robin access to the devices. Figure B-3 shows that the SCSI control unit is a polling channel. First, the SCSI card interfaces with Device 1, then 2 (the tape drive), then 3, then 4, and finally 8 (to look for more requests from the CPU), then back to 1 again. In each case, it either passes information to the device or asks the device if it has anything for it.

You can mix disk and tape devices on the same channel. This may or may not be a good idea, but usually is the cause of performance problems. Often a tape drive is asked to process large volumes of data in a sequential manner. Thus, when the SCSI device polls the tape device, it might be opening a data-box and spend large amounts of time processing that device. **All other devices** wait until the processing of the request is completed. If your database I/O request is on Device 1 while a large set of blocks is coming off the tape drive, the I/O may be delayed. What if the I/O was delayed 1/2 second? What if 20

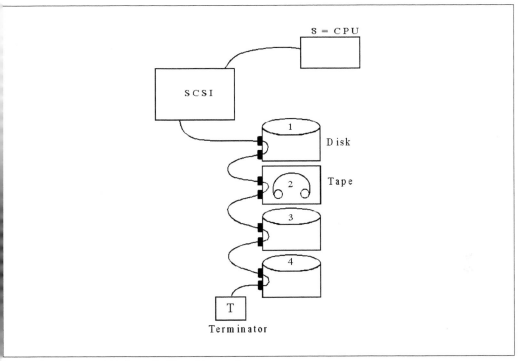

Figure B-3. Control Unit as Polling Channel

Since SCSI is a polling architecture, try not to have fast devices (disks) on the same SCSI as slower devices (tapes) because it will go to the fast one, then the slow one and delay the faster devices.

I/Os were required for a request? The I/O *delay* time would be 10 seconds.

Separation

Figure B-4 shows what most people do to minimize the effect of sequential devices. They put the slower devices, such as CD/ROM and tape drives, on a separate SCSI channel.

This is similar to the lines at the grocery store where there are regular checkout lines for people with full carts and express lines for people who have 10 items or fewer. Polling devices are a lot like that. If one person has a transaction that takes far more time than others, the queue will build up until that one transaction completes.

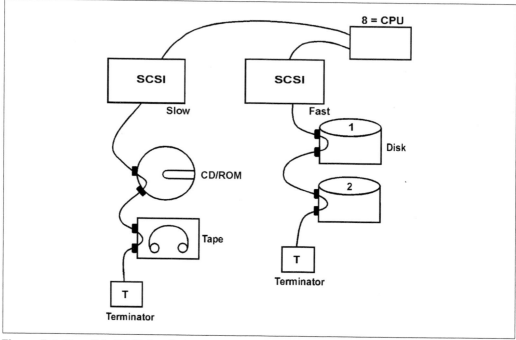

Figure B-4. Possible SCSI Configuration
You may find that you must move slow devices such as CD/ROMs and tapes to a separate SCSI card. A small price for a card may give you big performance benefits in reduced response time.

Length Considerations

Figure B-5 shows a near-full SCSI channel. Cabling lengths are important. Cables from the SCSI card to the terminator cannot be more than 18 feet for most implementations. Like the mainframe, you cannot just total the cable lengths between boxes. Look at the plugs into Device 1. Note that the cable seems to go inside the device. The reason is that you must measure the length of the travel of the electrons, not just the length of the extension cables. Each device uses some number of inches or centimeters to handle the electrons.

You can put hard disks (direct access storage devices), CD/ROM, or tape devices on a SCSI channel. You should ask yourself what length should be added to the total length for each device. Then you can add it to the length of the cables.

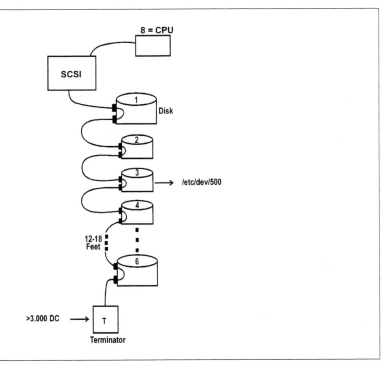

B

Figure B-5. A Near-Full SCSI

*SCSI has length limitations. Yes, you can put 8 to 32 devices on a channel, but in most cases the total
length of the cables is 12-18 feet. (Some newer architectures extend this, but there still is SOME
limitation.) How long is too long? Some SCSI implementations require exact voltages all the way to the
last device (as indicated by 3.000 volts at the end). If the length is too long, you may get channel overruns
and timeouts.*

Between 12 and 18 feet, you may start to get what
mainframe people call *channel overruns*. When this
happens, everything stops while the channel goes into
error recovery to fix the problem (probably just
starting the operation over again). For you hardware
buffs, the voltage at the terminator must be *over 3.000
volts DC* (that is why I wrote "3.000 V DC" to indicate
it cannot be 2.9 volts, for instance). One solution is to
have an *active terminator* to tap into the voltage of the
device and boost the voltage on the cable to at least
3.000 volts.

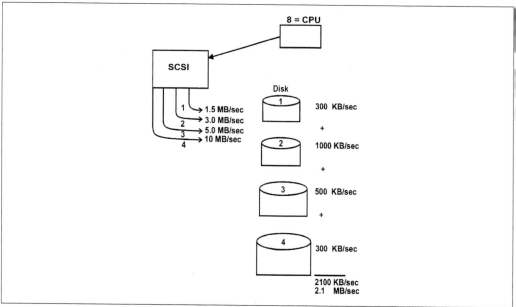

Figure B-6. Information You Need to Decide

Even if you don't have too many devices as measured by feet or meters, you can overcommit the SCSI channel. As you add devices, the speed of the devices may give you an indication you will have problems if all of the devices are busy.

Throughput

Figure B-6 shows the information you will need to decide when you have filled up a SCSI channel. You need to know the type and speed of the channel.

In this example, the total rate of all devices is 2.1 MB per second. If the SCSI is a 1.5-MB-per-second channel, it will cause problems if the buffers and cable cannot keep up.

Transfer Rate

A second piece of information you will need is the transfer rate of each device on the channel. The first two types of SCSI usually have 5 MB/sec rates. SCSI-3 usually runs between 5 MB/sec and 10 MB/sec, but the cable length is reduced to about three meters. The newest SCSI are fiber channels and can run at 20-25 MB/sec.

When you look in vendor tables, samples are given of possible *maximum data rates* for devices. Again, as part of your inventory, you will need to determine what the rate is.

Now just add the data transfer rates of all of the devices together. Now for the hard part.

What will be the peak and sustained data transfer rate? If your SCSI channel is 2,100 KB per second (2.1 MB per second), could you operate on a 1.5 MB channel? Maybe. Maybe not. What if you installed a 10 MB/second SCSI? Maybe. Maybe not.

This is where you must decide if you want to model or measure performance. If you want to model performance, you need to decide what your variables were and pass them through a mathematical model to give the channel a yes or no.

B

If you want to measure performance, you need to use a software monitor to measure the SCSI channel and decide if the data transfer rate exceeded the capacity of the channel.

You probably will want to use a combination of modeling and measuring, depending on your situation.

Where to Look

As you probably have seen, each UNIX implementation has different structures. One of the things you can do to learn how the system is configured is to look at available system information. Here are some suggestions.

Device Information

The place to begin is the directory /dev/dsk (or just/dev) and /dev/rdsk subdirectories. If you do the long form of the ls-e command on these two, you will find the place UNIX looks for information about the devices. The output looks like a file listing except that the device number replaces the byte count. The number consists of a major number. For example:

```
ls -l /dev/dsk
```

```
brw- - - 2 root sys   10,0 Sep 10 12:00 dev0s0
```

The first character, *b*, indicates that this is a block device, it is device zero, and it is accessed by the 10th device driver. To see what device drivers you have installed, look in /etc/master.d/README and find the values in ExternalMajorNumbers.

SCSI Information

Most vendors provide tables for their hardware. For example, a kernel variable called *scsi_options* probably shows the values defined for each device.

Sysinfo

The Internet provides many useful sources you can use to gather information about your system. You, of course, must know and be able to compile the C source code. One such source is the University of Southern California. The sysinfo program provides various pieces of information about the hardware and software configuration. It seems to compile easily and run on all platforms. It is written by Michael Cooper (mcooper@usc.edu). To get your copy, try file transport protocol (ftp):

```
ftp usc.edu
Name (your name): anonymous
cd /pub/sysinfo
get [put the names you want here]
```

Summary

You must know your hardware as part of any performance management exercise. You must know the speed of the interface of the channel and all devices attached. You must know how they act.

This chapter is really just the beginning. You will see new advances in disk technology coming faster and faster. Hopefully, these concepts will help you ask the right questions of your hardware vendor to get the most bang for your buck.

Glossary

The following is a glossary of UNIX terms from the UNIX platform, Landmark's **The Monitor** for UNIX (TMON for UNIX), or *PerformanceWorks*/SmartAgents for UNIX.

AFS
Project *Andrew's File System*. This was the first file system that added buffers in the local or home system to minimize network traffic.

(average) response
Response is one of the most widely discussed topics relating to performance. Response time within TMON for UNIX is the delay between a terminal read completion and the first character returned. This does not take into account the fact that many "logical" transactions involve multiple terminal reads, but this value provides a good yardstick.

background
Generally used to describe a task that can be started and performed without interaction from the terminal. Usually a program run from a shell with an ampersand (&) as the last character of the shell command so that it will run "unattached" from the shell.

batch
Usually used to describe a task that will run for an extended period with no terminal user intervention. A batch process is distinguished by an ampersand (&) as the last character of the command or line in an executable file. An example is a file containing UNIX shell commands that is required to perform some function to be run by means of the <filename>& shell command. In practice, any task that requires more than a few seconds to process should be included in this definition. The broad definition can perhaps be stated as "not interactive" and should include compiles and queries, since they usually exhibit this processing characteristic. *Batch* jobs also

can be started or scheduled to run using the UNIX `cron` or `at` facilities. Some background jobs can be classified as *batch* if they require no user interaction and use some minimum amount of CPU time.

block

The largest amount of data a UNIX file system will allocate contiguously. The size typically varies from 1K to 8K. The file system block size is different from the physical block size of a disk drive in the mainframe environment.

blocked

Many resources of the system cannot be shared. To maintain integrity of the resource, objects such as file directories must be accessed exclusively. Because of the multiuser nature of the UNIX environment, conflicts often occur. When a process is kept from continuing because some other process has exclusive use of a resource, the waiting process is said to be *blocked* by the process that currently owns the resource.

blocked I/O

I/O operations performed in blocks. A block is typically in the range from 1K to 4K. Many random-access devices such as disks can perform I/O only in block size increments (one or more sectors). The UNIX file system provides a byte stream abstraction on top of the disk subsystem and performs block I/O transparently for the user.

bottleneck

At any point, the reason the task being performed is not being processed at a faster rate. It may be that the CPU is not fast enough, the disk drives are too slow, or some other resource is under contention.

buffer

A storage area used in the transfer of data during an I/O operation.

buffer cache

The UNIX system maintains a collection of buffers within the kernel that are used as cache for user I/O requests. The buffers are not dedicated to a single process, but are shared globally. The buffer cache features read-ahead and write-behind and provides synchronization between processes opening the same file.

busy

Generally, any task that is actively processing. More specifically, the times when a resource is being used. This can be the CPU being busy or a disk controller being in a busy state. Often, this busy state is further defined with the actual activity the resource is currently processing, such as "busy processing disk cache instructions."

caching

A technique used to improve the performance of some storage resource. In most cases, if part of a storage area is required now, another part of the area near the first one will be requested soon. This physical proximity of storage requests is relied on to allow a smaller yet faster resource to attempt to appear as if it is the larger and slower resource. UNIX disk caches allow a file system implemented as a byte stream to be provided on top of a block device. Two relevant examples are the use of higher speed memory or registers to improve the performance of main memory and the use of main memory to speed up disk or other slow device access.

canonical transaction

A single "logical transaction" typically ending in an end-of-line transmission. In UNIX, line editing, retype, echo, and other functions are not performed by an application reading from the terminal; rather, they are performed by the terminal device driver. The line of input is transferred to the application on receipt of an end-of-line character, most commonly the ENTER key, between the completion of a terminal read and the initiation of the next write.

channel

Usually a hardware interface facility that provides a unique path for communication between a device and the computer main memory. In most cases, *channel* implies a dedicated conduit. In some cases, devices must share part of the route with some other hardware communication routing.

child process

Any process created by another process. The creating process is termed the *parent*.

configure

The act of specifying the structure, size, or type of some aspect of the system. It can be used to describe the act of specifying the sizes of the various system tables, the hardware devices connected to the system, and the default options within TMON for UNIX.

context

See hardware context.

control block

Some predefined data layout used to keep track of some entity. Common uses for *control blocks* within the UNIX environment include such things as the status of a file and the current status of some hardware device such as a terminal port.

CPU

Central processing unit. This is a hardware concept common to all computing environments. It is the part of the physical machine that performs (or executes) the program instructions to add, subtract, or move data, or provide control instructions. These instructions are executed sequentially until a branch is taken or some other part of the computing system takes over control of the processing. If you have one CPU in the "computer," then one process can be running at any instant. *See multiprocessing.*

current interval

A term within the TMON for UNIX environment that refers to the time period to which the currently displayed sample relates. By default, this is defined as 60 seconds in TMON for UNIX. A new interval also can be defined simply by pressing the Interval soft key and entering a value between five seconds and 59 minutes. The current interval is automatically overridden any time you press a keyboard key.

current offset

As a file is being processed, the file system maintains a number of characteristics about the file and its usage. One important thing being tracked is the relative character or byte position within the file most recently referenced. In the case of files accessed serially, this pointer advances from the start of the file to the end of the file. In the case of files accessed randomly, this pointer will jump around the domain of the file as the processing randomly accesses the data.

current process

In the UNIX environment, multiple processes are typically runnable at any given time. Since there is usually only one CPU within the computer, only one process can actually be running at any moment. The process that is running at an instant in time is referred to as the *current process*.

daemon process

One of the three basic categories of processes within UNIX (the other two are user and kernel). Performs systemwide functions such as network administration, print spooling, paging, or buffer flushing. *Daemon processes* are characterized by having no association with a particular user or terminal. The term *daemon* is sometimes pronounced like the word "demon," but more recently has been pronounced "dA-mon." (Maybe it's the politically correct crowd again!) The mainframe equivalent is *started systems task*.

See also kernel process and user process.

DFS

Distributed File System. This is the file system defined by the Open System Foundation (OSF) that is similar to AFS.

disk buffering

A technique used to improve the performance of the disk subsystem. In most cases, if any disk area is required now, another part of the area near the first one will be requested soon. This physical proximity of disk requests is relied on to allow a smaller yet faster resource to attempt to appear as if it is the larger and slower resource. It is really a logical extension of blocking and buffering techniques handled by UNIX on a systemwide basis.

disk freespace

Disk space within the UNIX environment is managed in a very dynamic manner. When disk space is required, it is found from a pool of unused space in the file system. When a file is deleted, the space that the file occupied is given back to the pool of freespace. Generally, about 10% of the total capacity of each file system is available as freespace. The freespace in a file system can be determined by the df command or the Freespace function of TMON for UNIX.

disk inode

A control block that is an entry within the physical file system used to store the essential information about a file including owner, permissions, and disk layout.

dispatcher

A procedure within the UNIX kernel that provides the function of determining which process within the system will be switched to next. Every time a process cannot continue (for example, it is waiting for I/O or is blocked), it calls a procedure to inform UNIX of this fact. As part of this pause procedure, the dispatcher code is initiated. The functions of the dispatcher code are to adjust the priority of the pausing process based on the niceness value and the resource utilization of the process and then to search for the process with the highest priority on the system that is ready to run (which may be the same process again!). Other factors considered by the dispatcher are available memory and run queue size.

fault

Used in caching techniques when reference is made to the cached resource, and the area being referenced is not contained in the cache and must be accessed from the slower media. It is essentially a "cache miss." Also used within the memory manager functions of UNIX to refer to a memory reference that is not in main memory and must be brought in from virtual memory or disk. Virtual memory techniques are really a form of caching.

file mask

The set of permissions not provided for newly created files and directories.

file system

Generically, the services provided within UNIX that facilitate the allocation of secondary memory for efficient storage and retrieval of data. *File systems* are hierarchical in structure and include all the files known to UNIX.

freespace

The memory management routines perform the services of finding main memory space to satisfy requests. This is the space obtained by taking memory from other processes in an attempt to distribute memory evenly among requesting processes.

function

A major TMON for UNIX feature you can use to explore the product screens.

gid

Group identifier. The number assigned to a particular accounting group. It typically ranges from zero to some maximum value, depending on the UNIX system.

global

A generic term used to describe something that is shared by all or many processes on the system. It can be used to refer to such things as overall system resource utilization.

group

Within UNIX, a collection of users who are related. This is done either during the creation of the user or later as a change to the user. *Groups* can be conveniently used to control file access through group access privileges. A *group* also can be used for accounting and security.

HFS

High-Sierra File System or hsfs. This is the file system used for UNIX systems on CD/ROM that extends the ISO 9660 specification to allow long (greater than eight characters and three characters).

I/O

Input-output.

idle

A possible state of a resource. The most common example is the CPU resource. When the CPU cannot continue processing either because there is no work to do or the processes that might continue cannot continue until some other event such as a disk I/O completion occurs, the CPU is said to be *idle*. When studying a system, you should know not only that the CPU is idle, but also why it is idle. Many TMON for UNIX screens provide information that relates to causes of idleness of either the system as a whole or an individual process. The term "idle" by itself is usually used to describe a situation where there is currently nothing to do.

incore

The condition that some memory object is actually resident in main memory as opposed to being out on disk where it would require swapping in or paging in before it could be accessed. It denotes the ability to access the object very quickly (at main memory speed).

incore inode

An incore and expanded copy of an inode, kept in memory while its file is open; used as a buffer for the disk inode, which is rewritten to the disk after the file is closed. This is the most up-to-date copy of information about a file.

inode

The control block that describes a file and its owner. It contains information about the location of the data blocks on the storage media assigned to this file. *See also disk inode and incore inode.*

interactive process

A process that has a terminal as its standard I/O device. It is commonly used to describe any process that is part of a session, although many processes run from terminals are really better described as batch processes.

Internet Control Message Protocol (ICMP)

A host-to-host communication protocol used on the Internet for reporting errors and controlling the operation of the Internet Protocol.

Internet Protocol (IP)

The network-layer communication protocol used in the Internet. *IP* is responsible for host-to-host addressing and routine packet forwarding, as well as packet fragmentation and reassembly.

interprocess communication (IPC)

A facility for communicating between cooperating processes.

interval

Used within the TMON for UNIX environment to refer to the length of time that elapsed before data collection was performed.

kernel

The central entity of the UNIX operating system. It is used to refer to the core facilities of UNIX, including the services for basic I/O, process control, CPU scheduling, memory management, and interprocess communication. The kernel is different for each UNIX platform (that is, IBM AIX, HP, SunOS, or Sun/Solaris).

JFS

Journal File System. JFS is most widely used by database systems.

kernel level

Processes that are currently executing code or using services supplied by the UNIX kernel. Implies a privileged mode of operation.

kernel process

One of the three basic categories of processes within UNIX. A process the UNIX operating system may start as part of its normal working set. In MVS, these are started systems tasks such as GRS and CONSOLE. Since each UNIX implementation is different, you may want to look at all processes just after your system is booted and then after all users are off, just before shutdown. *See also daemon process and user process.*

lofs

Loopback File System. This seems to be a file system that allows programs to input and output data quickly and easily.

logging

The act of recording information onto some semipermanent media so that it can be referenced later. In the case of TMON for UNIX, it refers to an option that collects the raw data upon which the interactive screens are based so that it can be reviewed later for generating usage trends or investigating specific situations after the fact.

logical request

A request for some resource that may have been satisfied without actually referring to the resource itself. An example of this is within the file system. The typical program references files by requesting that a particular record be transferred either to or from a file. Within the file system itself, user read and write requests are grouped into logical block requests from the disk subsystem that performs real or physical block requests called "blocks." By doing this, the file system reduces the number of times the relatively slow exchange of data between main memory and the disk media must be performed. Each read or write request is called a *logical request*, while the actual transfer of data between main memory and the physical media is called a *physical request*. When you are accessing files serially, there will be many logical requests for each physical request because of the blocking factor of the file.

main memory

The high speed semiconductor storage area within the CPU. It is the memory area used to store instructions and data while they are being processed.

memory fault

When a reference is made to any data in virtual storage and that data is not currently in main memory, a request must be made to the memory manager to bring into main memory the page that contains that data. In the meantime, the calling process must stop until the memory manager has completed its task. This sequence is called a *memory fault*. In UNIX, the process that causes a fault performs the I/O required to bring the page into memory. Of the memory manager's functions (vhand and sched), vhand takes pages from the user, writing them to disk if they no longer reflect the content of the source. sched performs swap-in and swap-out of entire process memory.

memory manager

The component of UNIX that manages the main memory resource. The task of this part of the operating system software is to keep the most frequently used pages of memory in main memory and to handle the transfer of memory between main memory and virtual memory as needs change.

memory shortage

Insufficient real memory to handle the total working set of all active processes.

memory units

The cumulative charge for memory usage. This value is calculated by averaging the number of private pages associated with a process plus its share of shared pages.

modifier

The qualifier to a particular function within TMON for UNIX. The various *modifiers* within a given function provide a means of further defining the specific area of interest within the general area defined by the function. Modifiers consist of the system/user selection, the active selection, and a set of process filters.

module

A defined set of kernel-level routines and data structures used to process data, status, and control information on a stream. It consists of a pair of queues (read and write) and communicates to other components in a stream by passing messages.

NFS

Sun's Network File System. The files on this file system reside on a spindle attached to another UNIX system. The files are *remotely mounted.*

niceness

UNIX processes can change their dispatching priority by using the `nice` command. The value passed is a number from 0 to 39, with the default being 20. The higher the value, the lower the priority after the `nice` command. Under UNIX System V Release 4, the `nice` command works only on time-sharing processes.

overhead

Processing that must be done as part of the operation of UNIX, but that has no direct applicability to a particular process. Most often used to describe the CPU activity that cannot be assigned to a particular function, but is still consuming part of the total capacity of the CPU.

An example of this type of CPU *overhead* is the processing required to handle interrupts from peripheral devices. In a broader sense, all processing that is not related to the actual instructions for the program(s) being run could be considered to be *overhead*, although the term is seldom used in such a general sense. In UNIX, overhead time is not collected explicitly, as the time required to process interrupts is charged to the current process. Certain processes can be classified as overhead, such as the swapper, pager, and buffer flush daemon.

page
The smallest unit of memory that UNIX utilizes. *See also paging.*

paging
In many versions of UNIX, main memory is arbitrarily divided into pieces ("pages"), so the memory management functions of the kernel can attempt to keep the most frequently referenced memory in main memory while relegating the less frequently used memory locations to disk media. This also is referred to as *demand paging,* referring to the process of loading a page from virtual storage into main memory on demand.

parent process
In an environment in which processes create other processes, the process that creates another process is said to be the *parent* of a new process. An example of this is when a user starts a program from the shell. The process that is created becomes the *child* of the shell, and the shell is the parent process.

pcfs
PC/DOS File System. This file system is when a UNIX system is going to access a PC-based spindle.

physical request
See physical transfer.

physical transfer

Within the file system, many requests for data transfers can be satisfied from within main memory without actually transferring data between main memory and the peripheral device. In cases where a request cannot be satisfied from main memory and an actual transfer takes place, the occurrence is referred to as a *physical request* or a *physical transfer*. Since physical transfers are the limiting factor in peripheral device performance, we are often attempting to reduce the number of physical transfers necessary to satisfy the logical requests.

pid

Process identifier. The number assigned to a particular process and used within UNIX to identify the process uniquely and concisely. One of the few outward appearances of this number is the first column in the output from the ps command.

pipe

A facility for communicating between cooperating processes. A *pipe* is a unidirectional byte stream connecting one or more processes.

priority

All processes within the UNIX environment are assigned a numeric priority that determines in what sequence they should be executed when they are competing for a resource of the system. The lower the numeric value of the priority, the higher the level of importance.

process

The unique execution of a program by an individual user at a specific point in time. In the UNIX system, the three general categories of processes are daemon, kernel, and user. Each process is assigned a unique integer called a *process ID (PID)*. This number is a wrap-around number. Just like MVS, the first numbers are assigned as system functions start up. For most UNIX systems, these are sched, pageout, fsflush, and kmdaemon.

process group

The set of related processes created by the same parent. A process is free to create its own *process group*.

process state

Whenever a process is doing or not doing something on the system, it is considered to be in a particular "state." Examples of *process states* include sleep state, ready state, and swap state.

process switch

A process is "switched" when it changes between running in user mode to kernel mode and back.

process tree

Within UNIX, one process can create one or more other processes called "child processes." These created processes can themselves create processes, having "children" of their own. The family of processes that is created in such an environment makes up a *process tree*. UNIX itself consists of a number of processes arranged into a family, one of which is the parent of all processes (sched). Similarly, the shell process that you interact with when you log in is the parent of all processes subsequently created by you.

program file

The disk resident file that contains the processing instructions for a particular program in a format that can be loaded and run by UNIX.

prompt

The character that is displayed as an indication that some input is expected from you. For instance, the prompt that the Bourne shell uses when it expects you to issue a command is the dollar sign ($). This prompt can be changed by modifying a shell-specific variable (usually *PS1* or *PS2*).

queue

Within UNIX, there are many instances in which access must be serialized for some resource. When this serialization occurs, those tasks waiting for the resource are kept together in a *queue*, a linked list maintained for the particular resource. Other queues are used to buffer output to a serially accessible device. When the length of the list is other than zero, the resource is being "queued up" — the waiting tasks are queued for the resource.

queue stream

A data structure that contains status information, a pointer to routines for processing messages, and a message queue.

real memory

In the context of system performance, usually used to refer to memory locations currently resident in main memory in contrast with the abstraction of virtual memory, which may require access to disk media.

region

The logical areas into which the kernel divides the virtual address space of a process. It is a contiguous area of address space.

register

Implementations of a storage medium that have an access speed faster than main memory locations.

related process

All processes are children and, as with people, all processes that have children are *parents*. Unlike people, a single parent can create a child by using the fork system call. All the children created by a parent are called *siblings*. The parent and its children are all related and form a family tree. It is defined by three pointers in the proc structure. This is similar to the *task control block (TCB)* structure in MVS.

One example of a process family tree is the shell environment, in which the shell is the *process group leader* of the related group.

resource

Anything that is used to do work. System performance focuses on the consumption of resources to locate the current limiting resource so that it can be increased in capacity or the demand can be reduced. Resources include the CPU, main memory, disk drives, available time in the day, and data files.

response time

In general, the time required by the system to produce the correct action or output for a given input. There are two basic methods for measuring response: the time from the completion of the terminal read operation by the program until the first character of output and the completion of the response from the time the prompt is redisplayed. Within TMON for UNIX, all response figures report using the former method.

response to first character

The elapsed time between the completion of a read operation and when the first output character is processed. The completion of a read operation is the end-of-line character (the ENTER key) when the terminal is in canonical mode or any character when it is in raw mode. This is the response measure used within TMON for UNIX.

response to prompt

The elapsed time between the completion of the read operation and when the program is available to receive the next input. The completion of a read operation is the end-of-line character (the ENTER key) when the terminal is in canonical mode or any character when it is in raw mode. This is the response measure used within TMON for UNIX.

RFS

AT&T's Network File System. This file system is similar to Sun's NFS.

run queue

The number of processes residing in memory and ready to run that only are waiting on CPU allocation to continue.

sample interval

The frequency with which a new data sample is collected and processed by TMON for UNIX.

script

A series of one or more shell commands that have been stored in a file and can be used as a group by simply naming the file at the shell prompt.

sector

The minimal amount of disk space readable by the disk drive. Typically, one sector represents 256 or 512 bytes.

service level

As it pertains to the study of computer system performance, an attempt to quantify the performance of a system. Usually defined based on a results-oriented indicator such as response time. In some instances, it is used to refer to the basic availability of the system itself.

shell

The program started on a user's behalf at login. It is the terminal interpreter program that interfaces the user to the operating system. It accepts input commands from the user and implements interfaces to UNIX utilities. There are a number of shells you may be using. The *C shell* (uses the /bin/csh command) is the base shell. The prompt you will see is customized to the directory you are in (similar to the pg command in PC DOS). The *Korn shell* (uses the /bin/ksh command) is another version; the prompt is the number sign (#). The *Bourne shell* (uses the /bin/sh command) is still another version and the prompt is the dollar sign ($). To see what version you are using, type *echo $SHELL*. To change your login default (across logouts) to the one in use, type *chsh*.

sibling

A process created from the same parent process as another child process.

socket

An endpoint of communication in the socket interprocess communication model. It is the data structure used to implement the socket abstraction.

spooler

A facility within UNIX that allows the logical sharing of serially usable devices. Most commonly used to facilitate output to printers where the data is actually written to an intermediate disk and then printed when the printer is available. A side benefit of this is that a program can spool a long report to disk and then continue with other work while the actual printing takes place at some other time.

state

See process state.

streams

A general, flexible facility for the development of UNIX communication services. It provides a full-duplex processing and data transfer path between processes, stream drivers, and stream modules.

swap-in

A procedure within the memory management routines of UNIX that brings the process context swapped out to disk in a previous swap-out operation back into memory so that it can be scheduled to run.

swapping

Involves the complete removal of the executable process context. Once a process has been swapped out, it cannot be scheduled to run until it has been swapped in again.

switched in

When the UNIX scheduler makes a decision to assign the CPU resource to a particular process for a period of time, that process is said to be *switched in* (or scheduled). During the course of the life of a process, it will be launched many times. The dispatcher typically will make a decision about which process

Glossary

should be launched and then perform a launch many times in a single second.

system call

A call to a kernel procedure.

system process

At the time the system is first started, one of a number of processes created to provide certain service functions. This process and those subsequently created for other like functions are termed *system processes*.

thrashing

Severe memory shortage, usually characterized by the system spending a high percentage of its available resources doing memory manager functions rather than performing more useful work.

transaction

In general, a unit of work that fulfills some purpose. Examples of transactions include adding a new customer and paying an invoice. These tasks usually require a number of steps to be performed but are considered to be a single activity by the user. The definition within TMON for UNIX is limited. Since there is no real indication of how various activities should be grouped, a *transaction* is defined as the work done between one terminal read completion and the next. While this will not usually reflect reality, it does provide an index of activity that can be used for relative comparisons.

Transmission Control Protocol (TCP)

A connection-oriented transport protocol used on the DARPA Internet. *TCP* provides for the reliable transfer of data as well as the out-of-band indication of urgent data.

UFS

UNIX File System. The original file system that comes with standard UNIX operating systems.

uid

User identifier. The number assigned to a particular accounting user name. It typically ranges from zero to some maximum value, depending on the UNIX implementation.

useful work

Processing that works directly toward completing a task. Includes processing of the machine instructions contained in the user program and subprograms that are called explicitly, as well as file system access that results from direct user requests. This term is usually used to exclude the work done by the UNIX kernel just to keep the system running and performing general processing (overhead).

user

Anyone who logs into the system. It separates them from the operating system itself.

User Datagram Protocol (UDP)

A simple, unreliable datagram protocol used on the DARPA Internet. *UDP* provides only peer-to-peer addressing and optional data checksums.

user level

The state of a process when it is not currently executing kernel-level code or using kernel services.

user process

One of the three basic categories of processes within UNIX. A process initiated by a user of the system as opposed to the operating system itself. *See also daemon process and kernel process.*

vfs

Virtual File System. This is a generic name for standard UNIX file systems.

virtual

Usually the state of memory resources when they are not resident in main memory, but rather have been relegated to disk storage.

Glossary

virtual memory

Used to describe two things. First, the mechanism whereby the system manages requests for main memory space and maintains the most active memory users in main memory while keeping the less active users on disk where they can be swapped in as required. Second, the disk area where the storage resides. Stated more theoretically, it is an abstraction created by a combination of hardware and software that allows the transparent access of a set of memory addresses greater than provided by resident memory. The excess address space is usually backed by storage on a disk device.

wait state

Whenever a process is not actually running, the reason it is not running is recorded as part of the system table that manages processes. Usually the process is waiting for some event to occur such as disk I/O, a timer delay, or memory manager request completion. Of course, the process could be stopped, ready to run, but has lost its turn. *See also process state.*

Index

Index

Index

Robert H. (Bob) Johnson

Bob Johnson is Director of Technical Communications & Product Packaging for Landmark Systems Corporation. Mr. Johnson has more than 25 years data processing experience in large systems applications programming, systems programming, performance and tuning, and management of distributed systems. Bob has worked in large government and Fortune 500 company data centers. Bob has written two best-selling books on the IBM mainframe architecture: *MVS Concepts and Facilities* (ISBN 0-07-032673-8, Spanish 84-481-0092-1) is the largest selling book for McGraw-Hill's Jay Ranade series; *DASD, IBM's Direct Access Storage Devices* (0-07-032674-6) is used throughout the world to understand and tune DASD subsystems. Bob holds a BA in business administration, automatic data processing from George Washington University and the CTM and ATM awards from Toastmasters International.

Comments on this work can be directed to:

Robert H. (Bob) Johnson
c/o Landmark Systems Corporation
8000 Towers Crescent Drive
Vienna, Va., 22182-2700
Phone: 703-902-8232
Fax: 703-790-3391
E-mail: bjohnson@landmark.com